The
Holy Valley

and the

Holy Mountain

le Bézu
Rennes Les Bains
Rennes Le Château

I. M. Gabriel

First published 1994 by I. M. Gabriel

© 1994 by I. M. Gabriel

ISBN 99920-1-048-7

Front Cover:
The hill is called La Pique which recalls 'The finding
of the child Jesus in the Temple'.

Hurst Village
Publishing

Printed in England by Shinfield Printers, Hurst, Reading, Berkshire.

Contents

List of Figures

List of Photographs and early Postcards

1   Reproduced by kind permission of Nicole Dawe of Rennes Les Bains

2   Early Labouche Frères postcard reproduced by kind permission of Bernadette Suau, the Director of the Departmental Archives of the Haute-Garonne.

3   Reproduced by kind permission of Angelo Longo, Editore, Ravenna.

4   Reproduced by permission of 'Scala' Photographic Institute, Florence.

5   Elisée Burgat, Epicerie, Toulouse.

6   —

7   ERA, 11 Bd Voltaire, Narbonne.

8   L Escudié à Quillan.

9   M. J. Modète.

10   The Author.

Map   Excerpts from I.G.N. Carte Topographic 2347 1:2500 East and West (at the end of the book) reproduced by permission of the National Geographic Institute of France.
© I.G.N. Paris 1984. Authorization No 90 - 3080

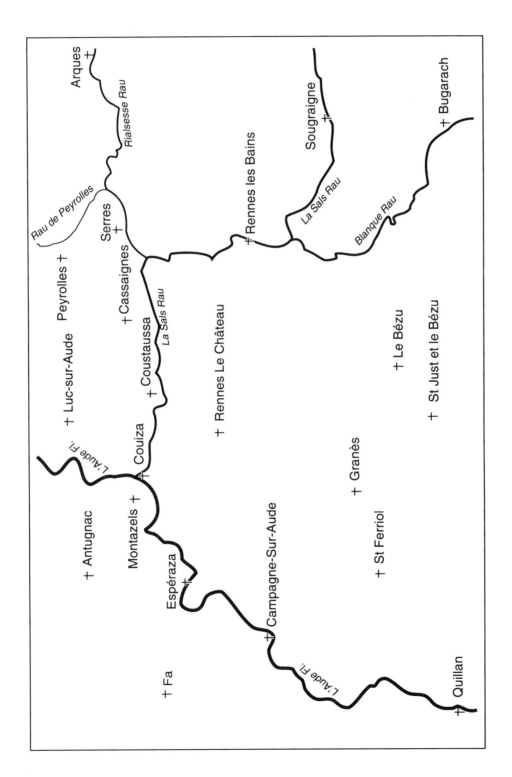

Fig. 1. Map showing local churches.

Introduction

That strange personage Abbé Bérenger Saunière of Rennes le Château seems to have left behind clues to something mysterious. Clearly it was not a 'treasure trail', as this would have been quite out of character for a priest. However, if there was a fabulous treasure, as some of our contemporary myth makers suppose, and if we try to follow the clues that Saunière is claimed to have done, then we have nothing very substantial to go on, and who would help us if he did know something about it?

The repeated allusions to the 17th of January, the memorial of St Anthony, and St Mary Magdalen, appear to be relevant, but to what do they refer? Well, I followed the clues left by Saunière and very soon discovered that there was a Cross laid out in the Valley of Rennes les Bains, a village which has a cross on its blazon, for it used to be known as the 'Valley of the Cross'.

The earliest type of topographical zodiac is that of Glastonbury where the fields have been shaped in forms to represent the figures of the constellations. This has Taurus setting in the west and dates it to that era. The next type are those which are divided into the twelve Signs, and have come down to us on the blazons or coins of their towns, and where they are not a direct portrayal of the constellation figures are something analogous. These seem mostly to belong to the era of Aries.

Jean Richer in his *Geographie Sacrée du Monde Grec* has described many of these in ancient Greece, which he found by studying the coins. Guy-Rene Doumayrou in his *l'esprit des lieux* depicts one that he found centred on Toulouse of the Aries era, which he inferred from the blazons of the towns.

The Cross that I found is probably unique, and of the latest type, as it is designed for the era of Pisces, the Christian era. It marks only the beginning of four Signs, but with its alignments marks many relevant Saints days, and also the Pentagrams of the elements in our Calendar, which are most enlightening. This Cross and the perfect equilateral Triangle made by the churches of le Bézu and the two Rennes led me to discover that the Pythagorean figures and their secrets (which Pythagoras obviously learnt from the ancient mysteries), were to be found here.

It became apparent that the key to the 'secret knowledge' of the past was hidden here, to preserve it for the future. The Cross, like a Mandala, is a catalyst that enables the well instructed student to recover this ancient wisdom.

I have found things what I think have never before been disclosed, such as the Microcosmic Woman, the Druidic Year and many facts about the Royal Art of Astrology.

This is the end of the Piscean era, and the beginning of that of Aquarius. At the beginning of each age a new culture, like the Phoenix, has to arise out of the ashes of the old. We have lost most of our esoteric traditional knowledge, and worse still, its manner of thinking. This has to be recovered so that the new religion of the age can be formed out of the best of the past.

To the sacred places of the earth, the lower class of sensitives have recently come by 'groping in the dark'. As they are generally in contact with lower astral entities, this has desecrated these sites. But this is the natural order of things, the strong negative influence builds up that attracts the 'lightning flash', and when we have invoked these higher beings, then with their presence, sacredness is restored.

The gardener manures the ground around the bush that produces the beautiful roses. That is why it is important for us to discover the secret wisdom of the past, and these Holy Places, to sanctify them again.

Source de la Madeleine, Rennes les Bains. (Postcard c. 1910.)

x

I Clues

The Holy Valley

The story begins with the arrival of the Rev Henri Boudet as the new rector of Rennes les Bains in October 1872, a young man in his prime at thirty-five years old, he was of a forceful and energetic disposition (being born under Scorpio on the 16th November 1873) who decided to make the best of his new position.

We know that he worked hard in his parish, and helped the sick who came to this Spa for a cure, Rennes les Bains had been famous for its healing hot springs and cold mineral springs ever since Roman times when it was one of the most important resorts in Gaul. There is every reason to believe that prior to the arrival of the Romans, it was the local sacred centre for the Pagan Gauls, for whom springs and rivers were especially sacred.

There has been found evidence of Roman buildings, broken votive statues, coins, etc. in the Valley, which suggests that there had been shrines erected to the Roman gods identified with the local Celtic deities, in order to incorporate this holy site of the Gauls into their own religion.

Rev Boudet recognised the importance of this ancient holy site as he indicated in a discreet manner in the book *La Vraie Langue Celtique* published in 1886, in this he describes the Valley of Rennes les Bains as a gigantic natural Cromlech (in Continental usage a stone circle) demarcated by various rocks on the surrounding hills, some of which he thought had been arranged by the Gauls.

On several of these he found engraved Celtic crosses which he believed to be the work of the first local Christians. Unfortunately, the main theme of the book which tries to explain the meaning of the local topographical words by "modern English" instead of Anglo-Saxon made it absurd. Today it has been suggested that this may have been a 'blind' and that some hidden meaning may lie behind explanations to hide his 'discovery', however romantic this apology may be, unfortunately it does not ring true, because he could have done this in a more subtle way without making such an error.

Nevertheless I do think that the Rev Boudet discovered a very profound 'secret' about this area, and its importance as a Druidic Nemeton; but not that of a fabulous treasure-trove in which so many people would like to believe.

It would appear that Boudet wished that this healing Spa could again be sanctified and become a holy place, perhaps in a similar manner to that of Lourdes, where the vision of the Beautiful Lady seen by the child Bernadotte Soubirous and attributed naturally by the church to the Virgin Mary, had made Lourdes a popular pilgrimage site. Perhaps he also had in mind the Apparition of the Holy Virgin to the children at Pontmain in the year preceding his appointment on the 17th of January 1871 (note the date).

It is interesting to note that there is a village called Soubirous about one and a half kilometres south south west of Rennes le Château.

The Holy Mountain

Then suddenly came support for the Rev Boudet and his interest in the archaeological history of the region, in 1885 the Rev Bérenger Saunière, a young and impulsive priest (born under Aries on the 11/4/1852) became Abbé of Rennes le Château, a small and obscure village on top of a beautiful but isolated hill with a broken-down church in a state of disrepair.

At first this must have been a great disappointment to the new incumbent who probably felt banished and despondent, then he found to his delight the Abbé of Rennes les Bains, the Rev Boudet, fifteen years his senior, enterprising, and a passionate amateur scholar of antiquity.

Boudet, perceiving Saunière's disillusionment in his decrepit church on the top of a mountain village 'at the rainbow's end', quickly realised that here was a great opportunity, if he could inspire him with his vision, then the area might become a religious centre like he thought it was under the ancient Gauls, where the sick would come not only for healing waters but with a sense of spiritual uplift, a place of pilgrimage, related this time to Our Lady.

The little church of Rennes le Château could be renovated in a very attractive manner, in order to draw pilgrims to the beautiful mountain village with its wonderful views of the surrounding countryside, it would become a popular excursion for the visitors to Rennes les Bains; also, clues to the Secret could be hidden in the decoration of the church, and partially revealed to some. It would then attract an educated and important type of pilgrim interested in the occult side of religion.

In some respects the Dream has come true, but unfortunately, through some sensational writers, many have been misled into thinking that the Golden Secret refers to material loot rather than one of a religious and philosophical nature.

So, as we know, Boudet fascinated Saunière with his parish, its ancient holy stones christianised with Celtic crosses, the legend of the Visigoths on his Holy Mountain and its history.

Astrologically however, as we have seen, Boudet was born under the sign of Scorpio the night house of Mars, whilst Saunière's sign was Aries the day house of Mars, thus initially Mars would have given an enthusiasm and impetus in common, however, as day is to night, and man to woman, opposite in nature, this would easily lead to misunderstanding.

Also in their horoscopes the sun in Scorpio is in a weakly discordant aspect with itself when in Aries, so it happened that the friendship between the Rev Boudet and the Rev Saunière was eventually ruptured. This seems to have occurred at the beginning of 1891, for the former did not attend the consecration of the Lourdes pillar at Rennes la Château on June the 21st (the summer solstice) of that year.

The question which arises is how did Saunière manage to raise such a large sum of money to enable him to repair and refurbish his church in an extravagant manner, to build the villa Bethany and the 'folly tower' Magdala and to have a very luxurious style of living?

It is generally accepted that he discovered a valuable cache within the church, and he was suspected of looking for others in his churchyard, for the locals made a complaint about his disturbing and removing the old tombs. This however would have been insufficient for his plans, but as usual the villagers presumed that he had discovered a substantial treasure.

Years later, after his death, the treasure lure was used by Marie Denarnaud, his house-keeper and beneficiary, to encourage Nöel Corbu to buy the domain Bethany, which he was going to turn into a hotel. She then resided in the presbytery, and it was agreed that before

2

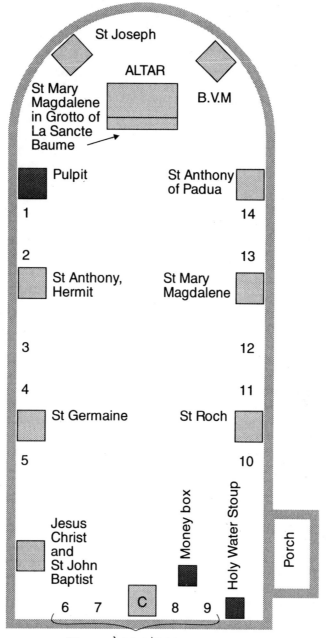

St Joseph

ALTAR

St Mary
Magdalene
in Grotto of
La Sancte
Baume

B.V.M

Pulpit

St Anthony
of Padua

1

14

2

13

St Anthony,
Hermit

St Mary
Magdalene

3

12

4

11

St Germaine

St Roch

5

10

Jesus
Christ
and
St John
Baptist

Money box

Holy Water Stoup

Porch

C

6   7   8   9

'Venez À Moi' Tableau

C = Confessional. 1-14 = Stations of the Cross

Fig. 2. Statues and features in Rennes Le Château Church.

she died she would reveal the Secret to him, unfortunately, in her dying moment she tried to but was physically unable. It was very natural that Mr Corbu should relate the tale about the Rev Saunière and great treasure to his visitors, since this appeared to be the great attraction and to many still is!

However, I think that it was more likely Saunière had become a Freemason, probably in order to join an occult society to which he revealed the real Secret told to him by the Rev Boudet, which was of great occult interest. In return, I think a few wealthy patrons could easily have paid for Saunière's expenses and arranged for him a substantial allowance. As Freemasonry was strictly prohibited to all Roman Catholics by many papal bulls, and was therefore a particularly serious misdemeanour in the case of a priest, this would not only explain his estrangement with Boudet that lasted until just before the latter's death, but also the persecution that he received from his new bishop elected in 1902. The bishop may well have had strong suspicions but was totally unable to bring any proof to bear, and therefore attacked Saunière's alibi that he had received large sums of money to perform countless Masses, which for a unknown country priest was highly unlikely.

The bishop accused him of trafficking masses and misusing these funds, and demanded a full account from Saunière as to how he came by these monies, but this he staunchly refused to reveal, which may bear out my surmise that he was too closely involved with Freemasonry, of which there are many traces in his church. For, surely, if he had discovered a secret hoard he would have disclosed it to the bishop and been duly rewarded by the Church?

If Saunière really did discover a substantial treasure there is certainly no reason to believe that he would have left us a Treasure Trail, and to try to follow his footsteps is hopeless for lack of evidence. Today many people think he found clues in the vertical flagstone commemorating the death of the Marquise of Blanchefort, Marie de Nègre d'Ables on the 17th of January, and the horizontal flagstone 'Reddis Regis' last seen by Mr Cros in 1908, both of which Saunière destroyed, but this seems to lead nowhere!

Nevertheless it does appear that the Rev Boudet was very interested in St Anthony the Hermit whose day is the 17th of January, and some have thought that he left some clues for us in his book, but if so these are very obscure. On the contrary the Rev Saunière seems to have left us some much easier clues in his church which may lead us to their Secret. Let us examine these:

The 17th of the Month

17th of January, St Anthony the Hermit

In most of the books dealing with the mystery of Rennes le Château it has been pointed out that the number 17 and the 17th of January, festival of St Anthony the Hermit who lived in the Egyptian desert, was indicated both by Boudet and Saunière, and is thought to be very significant. What is implied by this we are never told, and perhaps expressly so, as maybe the Secret of the two Rennes is known but is being jealously guarded by some modern occult society.

In the church of St Mary Magdalen at Rennes le Château, Saunière has placed a statue of St Anthony the hermit on the left side of the nave, and on the right side, exactly opposite, one of St Mary Magdalen. (See Fig. 2).

4

Thus, we have here on the left inside the church St Joseph, and St Anthony who was one of the first great founders of monasteries in the Church, suggesting the male laity and monks, similarly on the right are the Virgin Mary and Mary Magdalen implying the female laity and the nuns.

Here we will recall that according to the tradition of Provence and in the Golden Legend it is claimed that the Virgin Mary with Mary Magdalen, Mary wife of Cleophas, Martha, Lazarus, Joseph of Arimathea, and others travelled by boat from the Holy Land to Marseilles.

Mary Magdalen retired to the famous cave in the Sancte Baume mountains of Provence, where there had once been a holy wood of the Druids, St Mary Magdalen turns out to be the other major clue to the Secret.

17th day of the month and the Moon

Let us reflect on the meaning of the seventeenth day. In Ancient Egypt Plutarch tells us that it was on the 17th day of the month Hathor, when the sun was in the sign of Scorpio (approximately equivalent to November) that Osiris was murdered. Basically he was the river and fertility god of Egypt, and his murder symbolised the time when the river subsided and the inundation was over, also as a solar god, this is the time when the strength of the sun noticeably diminishes under the influence of the dark forces of winter and the 17th of Hathor was traditionally the day to begin to wear woollen clothes. In the Bible it was also on the 17th day of the second month that the rains of the flood began according to Genesis, and Noah's ark grounded on the 17th day of the seventh month.

In India the ancients had two types of Lunar month, in one the month started with the full moon, and in the other with the new moon. The Hindu month is also subdivided into the 'dark half' when the moon wanes, and the 'light half' when it waxes, in the former the nights get progressively darker, and in the latter lighter.

At the time of the astronomical new moon, when it has disappeared altogether from the night sky, the moon not having risen from the 'underworld' was thought to have died, and from Babylonia and Judea we learn of the rejoicing at the time of the 'resurrection' of the new moon and its birth with its reappearance in the evening sky. Doubtless the Babylonians and Sumerians saw in this the return of their fertility goddess Ishtar (or Inanna) from the underworld, and the Jews in later times blew the ram's horn when its reappearance with the sun in Aries marked the beginning of the first month of the year. The lunar month is around 29 days, so the months would be of 29 and 30 days alternately.

The moon attains its greatest glory when it is full, and gives the most light to the night sky, so the earliest type of lunar months probably started with the full moon.

This type of month which has come down to us in India, begins with the dark half followed by the light half. The Full Moon month was probably also the original one amongst the Jews, Gauls, and other ancient peoples who start the day in the evening after sunset, when the dark of night is followed by the light of day. Now in this month, taking it to be the round figure of thirty days, the first half is from the 1st to the 15th day, then with the disappearance of the moon on the sixteenth begins the second half.

As we have already noticed the astronomical new moon is not to be seen in the sky, but the crescent of the new moon appears twenty four hours or more just after sunset in the western sky, shortly afterwards to set below the horizon.

5

So the 17th originally stood for the birth of the Crescent Moon, shaped like a boat, and the ark of Noah similarly floated on the waters with the beginning of the flood on the 17th of the second month, ran aground on Mount Ararat on the 17th day of the seventh, in the same manner as the crescent moon might appear to rest on the mountains in the west. I think that the New Moon month came about with the supremacy of the Solar people, who worshipped the sun god, over those of the moon goddess. This tradition of the two distinct peoples who either worshipped the moon as a god or goddess, and those who worshipped the sun god or goddess, has also come down to us.

These solar people introduced the custom of reckoning the beginning of the day with the daily birth of the sun, or its reappearance from the underworld at sunrise, and therefore the beginning of the month with the appearance of the new crescent moon, and the bright half of the month.

With this New Moon month, the first day starts with the actual appearance of the crescent moon, generally following its disappearance at the astronomical new moon, which marks the bright half of the month and ends with the full moon on the 15th, in the second or dark half, which commences on the 16th, the decrease of the moon is not easily perceived until the second day, the 17th of this month.

Thus we see why the god Osiris was murdered on the 17th day of the month of Hathor, when the moon was seen to wane in his aspect as a lunar god. This is also the time of year when the inundation has passed its 'full', the level of the Nile falls, and the river returns to its banks in November, so figuratively Osiris as the river god, is enclosed in a coffin (or within its banks), by the god Set who then throws it into the river Nile, thus the day of the murder of Osiris, the 17th became a day of mourning and ill omen.

Plutarch informs us that the ancient Egyptians held a four day festival commencing on the 17th of Hathor on which they mourned, it represented the falling of the Nile and the return to its banks, the end of the pleasant northern winds overcome by the hot ones from the south, the lengthening nights and decreasing days, and the destitute appearance of the land and the fall of the leaves. The astronomical interpretation of this myth is that Taurus represents the Apis bull of Osiris, the symbol of fertility and Spring at the beginning of the Summer half of the year. Opposite is Scorpio and the beginning of Autumn and Winter, when Osiris 'dies', and his soul rests in Orion which is a paranatellon of Taurus, until the next Spring. In magic, which played a large part in primitive religion, the vitality of all living things was thought to be connected with the moon. When the moon waxed and grew bigger, the vitality increased, and when it waned and grew smaller, decreased, and then with its disappearance from the sky, there was the danger of death.

If a sorcerer wished to harm an enemy, he would cast his spells in the waning half, hence the 17th is the beginning of the evil period, the dark half of the New Moon month, however it was not necessarily always evil, for spells were done in this half to diminish the strength of wicked spirits which were thought to cause disease, and thus cure the patient. The ancients also believed that the moon waxed because it filled up with water, and waned because it released it. Therefore for the followers of the New Moon month the Flood of Genesis would be regarded as starting on the 17th, when with the waning phase the rains began to fall.

Probably the forerunner of Osiris as a lunar god (elsewhere than in Egypt which has very little rainfall except in the Delta) was most likely represented by a human sacrifice to the moon in order to release its rain upon the earth.

6

The 17th of March and the Cathars.

Though not directly connected as far as I know with the Secret of the two Rennes, nevertheless some of the following may prove to be quite relevant.

The Cathars of Montségur capitulated on the 1st of March 1244 and asked for two weeks grace before they left their castle, it has been suggested that because the Vernal Equinox of that year fell on the 14th of March (the Julian Year having gained against the true solar year), the Cathars then wished to celebrate a similar festival to the Manichean Bema, a sort of Easter rite following the Vernal Equinox.

Could it also have been the beginning of their religious year or the end of the old one?. In this case they may have had a year like the Ancient Egyptians and the Copts, which as we will see later appears to have been used in Europe. This has twelve months of 30 days each, and five Intercalary days (or six in a leap year). These Intercalary days which were outside the year cycle of twelve months were especially holy in Ancient Egypt, and we will discuss them later. The Castle of Montségur had five surrounding walls, which may possibly relate to these Intercalary days as well as obviously to the Pentagram and the five Elements of early philosophy. It has also been conjectured that the arrangement of these walls indicated by their alignments the solstices and the equinoxes.

Now assuming their year had five Intercalary days, starting with the first which coincided with the vernal equinox, and that they also represented the five elements, to which one could add the traditional vehicles of the different levels of consciousness, Body, Soul, Mind, etc. I have placed these elements in the order normally applied in the West and China, (In India Air follows Fire), and also the corresponding days of the month in 1244.

Vernal Equinox	March 1244			
14th	15th	16th	17th	18th
Monday	Tuesday	Wednesday	Thursday	Friday
Earth	Water	Air	Fire	Ether
Body	Soul	Mind	Heart	Spirit

Certain rites were probably performed on each of the five 'pentagonal days' corresponding to the four elements to be purified before the new year, the Cathars did not have much regard for baptism by water, but had a great respect for fire, the symbol of the baptism of the Holy Spirit.

We are told that after being asked in vain to renounce their Faith, two hundred and fifteen Parfaits and simple believers came forth from the Castle on the 16th of March towards evening, as evening amongst the Celts, Jews, and Christians, starts the new day, so this then was on the eve of the 17th of March which as we see from the above table corresponds to the element of fire. They then proceeded to the inevitable "burning to death" as heretics in the eyes of their opponents, but as true Christian martyrs overcoming the fear of pain and death, and believing in the consequential baptism of the Fire of the Holy Spirit.

The number 17 St Augustine tells us (Tract 123 in Joann: Ev:) represents the number 10 of the Decalogue, and 7 (Rev; 1 v4, 3 v1) the seven Spirits of God before the throne, or the Holy Spirit, thus 17 stands for the 'fulfilment' of the Law by the addition of Grace, the charismatic gift of the Spirit received in Christian baptism.

My supposition is that the Cathars had a year like the Copts, and as will be shown later the Druidic Year, with five Intercalary days, in the case of the Cathars the first of these fell on the vernal equinox. This is not so strange as may at first be thought when one bears in mind that the ancient 'legal year' (as opposed to the popular year) in France and most of Europe began with the 25th of March. This is the Feast of the Annunciation of the Virgin Mary, coming four days after the equinox in the Gregorian year, as Christmas and St John's birthday come three days after the solstices, but because the Julian year was too short, in the time of the capitulation of Montségur it had gained seven days from the Tropical year.

17th of January and obituaries

This was the date, as most of us know, of the death of the Marquise of Blanchefort, Marie de Nègre d'Ables of the noble family that once lived in the Château Blanchefort as the Lords of Rennes les Bains and its surrounding area, and finally resided in the Castle of Rennes le Château. The Reverend Saunière fell ill on the 14th and died on the 22nd of January 1917, though some claim that he had a stroke on the 17th, however we have 17 in the century if not in the month, and the 22nd as in the 22nd of July feast day of St Mary Magdalen, of whom he was so fond. His housekeeper and companion, Marie Denarnaud to whom he gave most of his possessions, made her will in favour of Nöel Corbu on the 22nd of July, doubtless deliberately on St Mary Magdalen's day, and died surprisingly enough thirty- five years after Saunière, within nine days of his memorial, on the 30th of January!

Elements

The Western and Chinese order of the Elements follows that which classifies them by their movement as follows :

Western and Chinese order of elements		
ETHER		
FIRE	rises	
AIR	rises and extends	
WATER	falls and extends	
EARTH	falls	

The Hindu order is that of their subtleness:

8

	Hindu order of elements	State
ETHER	Sound (subtle)	
AIR	Sound and Touch	Gaseous
FIRE	Sound, Touch and Form	Combustive
WATER	Sound, Touch, Form and Taste	Liquid
EARTH	Sound, Touch, Form, Taste and Smell	Solid

The five senses correspond to these.

The Pillar

As one enters the pathway to the Church of Rennes le Château, on the left side is a little oratory of the Virgin Mary. The statue which is a copy of Our Lady of Lourdes is supported by the so-called Visigothic pillar, which legend claims to be one of the two supports of the old altar which Saunière replaced in the church. It has been suggested that this ornate pillar

Side of the Pillar.

'Inverted' Visigothic Pillar.

was never in the church at all, but came from the ruins of another church in the village which was dedicated to St John the Baptist. This theory I think is supported by the fact that when Saunière held a little ceremony to bless the statue it was on the day of the summer solstice the 21st of June 1891, appropriately a Sunday, and the following Wednesday the 24th was of course the birthday of St John the Baptist. This Sunday was the occasion for the first communion of twenty-four local children; one cannot help thinking that Saunière deliberately chose 24 candidates representing the 24 half months of the year and the 24 Elders on the 24 seats around the throne of God (Rev. 4 v 4).

As was customary the cross on the pillar has the Alpha and Omega, the 'First and the last' under its arms (Rev. 1 v 18), these Greek letters had the numerical values of 1 and 24, their places in the alphabet, thus I think that Saunière imagined himself as the number 1, the priest of God with the 24 catechumens like the 24 Elders.

Let us examine the pillar, be it Visigothic, Carolingian, or even a fake, opinions vary. Firstly as many have observed, Saunière had the pillar with the cross on it deliberately inverted, the letters for Alpha and Omega being upside-down, also the longer arm of the cross from which comes the supporting rod, is at the top instead of being correctly, as one would hold it, at the bottom. This cross was most likely a copy of a metal one of the type carried in processions. The carving MISSION 1891 proves that this was done deliberately, and if it had been a mistake it could have been erased and carved again, as it a most scandalous act for a priest to allow the erection of an 'inverted' cross. This is therefore a most important clue to the solution of the Secret. This cross has often been compared to a Manichean one on a stele in the museum of Narbonne which has ten gems in each arm of the cross, and a central gem, I think that this can be taken to represent four Decans, or 40 days, which is approximately the time that a bright star or group of stars like the Pleiades in or near the zodiac, is obscured by the sun. Thus we have the 40 Dog Days of Summer (3rd July to 11th August inclusive) which marked the cosmic rising, or the time of the disappearance in the sun's rays to the reappearance in the night sky of Sirius in Canis Major, the Big Dog constellation. Forty is expressive of a period of trial or probation. Other periods of 40 days:

The 40 days	
1	that it rained in the legend of the Flood in Genesis
2	that Moses spent on Mount Siniai
3	the Jews wandered in the desert
4	Christ spent in the wilderness when tempted by the devil
5	of the Lent Fast
6	the days from Easter Sunday of the Resurrection to Holy Thursday or Ascension Day
7	also ATTA Gothic for Father with which the Pater Noster begins, adds up according to the older Greek valuation (A=1 T=19) to 40
8	the 40 hours from Jesus' death upon the cross and burial in the tomb

10

Our cross however is much more elaborate, we will examine it the right way up and find:

The cross at Rennes Le Château	
Arm of the cross	Number of Gems
TOP	23
BOTTOM	29
RIGHT	19
LEFT	18
	Total 89 Gems
at the CENTRE of the Cross	1 in a circle

These total 89 gems in the arms, and 90 in all — 90 suggests 90°, the right angle between the vertical and horizontal arms of the cross, the single central gem is like the Pole Star around which the others appear to move, and the Alpha the 'first' Greek letter.

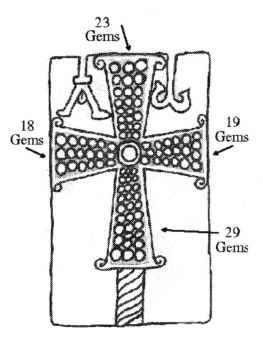

Fig. 3. Processional Cross of the Pillar (drawn the right way up).

- The Top arm of 23 gems plus the central gem gives 24, which suggests the 24 half months, of the bright and dark halves of the lunar year, the hours in the day, and the aforesaid Elders around the Throne. Thus Saunière's 24 children at the summer solstice when the sun is at its highest on the meridian, correspond to the upper arm of the cross, the vertical axis represents Spirit.
- The Bottom arm has 29 plus the Central gem giving 30, the days in the month.
- The Right arm and Central gem add up to 20, which might refer to half the 40 day period?
- The Left arm and Central gem gives us 19. This is the number of years in the Metonic cycle, when the moon's phases return to the same days of the same months, used to determine Easter.
- The two Horizontal arms together, excluding the Central gem, give 18 plus 19 totalling 37. This could be taken to show the 36 decans of the year, and the half decan of the Intercalary days as a round figure.
- Similarly the two Vertical arms of 23 plus 29 gives 52, the number of weeks in a year.

The decoration on either side of the pillar before it was reduced by Saunière probably represented two triangles and a diamond formed by a continuous rope of three straight cords, interlacing these is a continuous chain of gems forming two large circles and a smaller link. This pattern of triangles suggests amongst other things the three important positions of the sun on the meridian, highest at the summer solstice, in the middle at the equinoxes, and at its lowest the winter solstice.

From the above figures it would appear that our Visigothic column is connected with the year. Amongst occultists of the past there was a well known design of a man with his arms and legs outstretched forming a St Andrew cross, figured in a pentagram within a circle. This symbolises the Cosmic Christ of the Gnostics, the Microcosmic or Perfect Man, crucified by his descent into the five elements of the World of matter, and into time as the round of the year. Now Saunière, who was clearly very knowledgeable in occult symbolism, by reducing the pillar and inverting it, he leaves us with the pattern on either side of a diamond resting on the apex of a triangle. This gives us, with the five external points, if slightly flattened, a pentagram in which we can inscribe our Cosmic Christ. It is another important clue. Why is the cross deliberately inverted? Some may think of black magical practices, but I believe such imbecilities quite out of the question for the very independent and individualistic yet nevertheless very devoted priest.

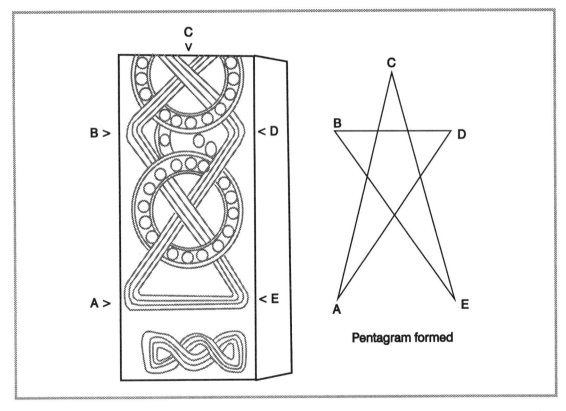

Fig. 4. Pillar Pentagram, Rennes Le Château.

There is a tradition, that out of great humility St Peter asked to be crucified upside down on the cross in reverence to Our Lord. St Peter's original name in Hebrew was Shimon, akin to Shimeon the tribe of Israel to whom the zodiacal sign of Pisces is generally attributed. Jesus gave him a new name, as his disciple, Cephas, Hebrew for a Rock which translates into Greek as Petros, and into Latin as Peter. But why was this name translated? Clearly so that its meaning should become perfectly apparent. He was the foundation stone of the Church, thus the Druids and other peoples would associate Christianity with their sacred stones which were similar to the ancient Hebrew Gilgals, and be more receptive to the new religion.

Figuratively St Peter is the living example of the Philosopher's Stone, and the Freemason's Perfect Ashlar. This therefore is another important clue.

Now the most significant question is why did Saunière have the Visigothic Pillar reduced, giving us the following dimensions — 75 cm high × 39cm wide × 40 cm deep— this gives a volume of 117,000 cubic centimetres. (75 × 39 × 40). As is customary in these cases we can ignore the zeros, which gives us the number 117, we can take this to mean either the 11th of the 7th (month), July, or the 1st (month) January, and the 17th (day). So here we have it, Saunière has again hidden the enigmatic day of St Anthony! In the case of the 11th of July, if one adds 11 days then we would have the 22nd, that of St Mary Magdalen to whom the church is dedicated. But why 11 days? Because the Hebrew alphabet has 11 plus 11 or 22 consonants, and 11 consonants are half of the alphabet we shall find later that from the day of St Mary Magdalen to that of St Anthony Hermit, there are 180 days or half of the Coptic year of 360 days (to which are added 5 Intercalated days.)

St Mary Magdalen is also indicated by the dual words PENITENCE PENITENCE carved on the capital above the Pillar which supports the statue of the Virgin Mary, dual, emphasising the feminine, and reminding us of the supreme female penitent, St Mary Magdalen.

The section area is 39 × 40 centimetres, or 1560 square centimetres, ignoring the zero we have 156, which may be interpreted as the 15th of the 6th (month), June, which is the day of St Germaine Cousin of Pibrac whose statue is on the left next to St Anthony the Hermit in the church. She was a young shepherdess and consequently is the patroness of young female agricultural workers. The section of the Pillar is horizontal, in line with the horizontal arms of the Cross, which represent the feminine axis of matter (so she is most appropriate here), the vertical arms of the Cross are masculine and symbolise Spirit.

Now the area of each vertical side of the Pillar is 40 × 75 centimetres which gives 3000 square centimetres, so here we have the number 3, a clear allusion to the Trinity, which is masculine, and also to the Trines of the Druids, and as we shall find later the Equilateral Triangle of le Bézu and the two Rennes.

The face is 39 × 75 centimetres or 2925 square centimetres, this might stand for the 2nd of the 9th (month), September, and the 2nd of the 5th (month), May. The Greater Eleusinian Mysteries started on the 15th of Boedromion, which ideally corresponds to the 2nd of September, for the Attic Calendar in theory started with the summer solstice, but in practice generally with the first new moon following it. This was the great drama of Demeter (whom the Italians identified with the corn goddess Ceres) who had lost her daughter Persephone to Pluto the god of the underworld. This represented the death of vegetation in the cold winter half of the year, and its resurrection and renewal in spring. The rites were especially concerned with the corn crops.

This is the subject that is of great interest to Freemasons and brothers of similar Occult Societies, even if this does not go so far as to implicate Saunière, it shows that he had a kindred affection. The 1st and 2nd of May are sacred to the Bona Dea or Maia, mother of Mercury, to whom the month is dedicated, she was worshipped by the vestal virgins, who also celebrated a secret festival on the 3rd and 4th. This is also the day, 2nd of May, of the great Christian theologian St Athanasius who was one of the four Fathers of the Orthodox Church.

On the face we have as the main feature the Inverted Cross. The area of the face being $2925 = 117 \times 5 \times 5$ square centimetres, again shows the 1/17 which we have seen stands for the day of St Anthony, and 5×5 suggests the two pentagrams **opposite** each other on either side of the pillar.

I think that this points to an upright and inverted pentagram centred on an inverted cross whose apexes are both in line with the main or vertical arms of the cross. This is indicated by the pentagrams on the sides, and finally we can assume that these two pentagrams are to be found centred on an Inverted Cross whose vertical arms have some connection with St Anthony the Hermit.

Supporting the Pillar is a rectangular stone resembling the flagstone of the Roman altar, which may have been the old altar table, thus this oratory as a whole would seem to be intended to symbolise the Pagan and Roman worship surmounted by the Pillar of the early Church, above which is the statue of Our Lady of Lourdes of the modern Catholic Church.

Above the statue is a canopy shaped like a building with an entrance flanked by two columns, which has a dome with two turrets, which may represent the Temple of the New Jerusalem.

The festival following a saint's day is often relevant, so just as we added the Central Gem to those in each arm of the Cross, let us add the morrows and their saints. Thus we have:

17 January	— St Anthony Hermit
18th January	— Chair of St Peter at Rome
15th June	— St Germaine
16th June	— St Quiricus[1] and his mother St Julitta, martyrs, 305 AD
2nd May	— St Athanasius
3rd May	— Invention of the Cross, when the Empress Helena[2] discovered Christ's Cross.
2nd September	— Greater Eleusinian festival of Demeter and Ceres, corn goddesses like Virgo in the zodiac.
3rd September	— St Stephen[3] the first Christian king, Patron and Apostle to Hungary, 1038 AD

1   The word Quiricus is obviously related to the latin Quercus an oak, which thus evokes the Druids.
2   St Helen the mother of the Emperor Constantine the Great, we will find that both are very relevant to The Holy Valley, in which we also have to discover the Cross.
3   St Stephen named after the Protomartyr of the Christian Church, to whom the church of Sougraigne east of the Valley is dedicated as The Invention of St Stephen, encouraging us to search.

14

Clues in the Church

We will take a cursory look for clues in the church. On the lintel of the porch are inscribed 22 letters, TERRIBILIS EST LOCUS ISTE 'This place is terrible', which was the cry of Jacob at Padam Aram where he erected a stone to God which was called Bethel (House of God). Here we may have an indication of the 'Cromleck' at Rennes les Bains. I will continue to use the word cromleck in the continental sense of a stone circle, because there is also a place called 'The Circle'which was probably once the site of a small stone circle.

As we enter the church, on our left we have the stoup held up by a magnificent Devil, who with his right hand forms a small circle between fingers and thumb, and places his left hand on his right knee, which is bent, thus forming with his arm, leg, and body, an oblong circle. The right hand with the small circle is placed above the large oblong circle, which suggests to me that he indicates the Circle at Rennes les Bains within the larger oblong one, or the Natural Cromleck of the Valley, which the Rev Boudet mentioned in his book. Le Cercle happens to be not very far from the Fauteuil du Diable (The Devil's Armchair). Above the stoup there are four angels making the 'sign of the cross' under a Celtic cross whose arms terminate in Fleurs de Lis, the cross thus indicates 3 times 4, or the number 12. Underneath the angels is a deliberate variation of the phrase IN HOC SIGNO VINCES, 'Par ce signe tu le vaincras', the addition of 'le' giving the total of 22 letters, which is the famous motto attributed to the emperor Constantine, though it originally read HOC SIGNO VICTOR ERIS as proved by the coins of Constantinus.

These four angels indicate the four arms of the cross, and probably also the four Cherubim which Ezekiel saw in the heavens, with the heads of a Man, Eagle, Bull and Lion; corresponding to the 'fixed signs' of the zodiac. Our angels in this case would be the regents of the four respective elements air, water, earth, and fire; the 12 points of the Fleurs de Lis indicating the 12 signs of the zodiac.

Stations of the Cross

On the northern side of the church we have:

Pulpit	— Station 1	Station 2
St Anthony Hermit	— Station 3	Station 4
St Germaine of Pibrac	— Station 5	

Opposite on the southern side:

St Anthony of Padua	— Station 14	Station 13
St Mary Magdalen	— Station 12	Station 11
St Roch	— Station 10	

Standing in the nave, let us imagine a saltire cross joining on one arm the statues of Magdalen and Germaine, and on the other those of Anthony the Hermit and Roch. Then if we imagine another line in the centre of the nave connecting the Altar in the east to the Confessional on the western wall, a Chi-Rho cross (Labarum of Constantine) is created out of this saltire cross.

Excluding the first and last Stations (1 and 14), and also those along the western wall (6 to 9 inclusive) we are left with eight Stations, numbers 2, 3, 4, 5, and 10, 11, 12, 13. If we were able to arrange these around a circle with the Chi-Rho cross, this would then suggest the twelve signs of the zodiac. (See Fig. 5.) This is another important clue.

Constantine and the Cross

I think it may be of interest to recall here what the Emperor Constantine told personally to the historian Eusebius of Caesarea. He and his British and Gallic soldiers saw a cross of light at noon over the sun with the inscription 'In this sign conquer', this they took for a good omen for they were all familiar with this pre-Christian cross, and it encouraged them for battle, they then went on to defeat the Roman Emperor and take Rome. It has been suggested that in reality a standard with the sacred solar wheel was used to rally the troops, for this was venerated by the Gauls, afterwards a loop was added to the top of the symbol to turn it into the Monogram of Christ.

The Chi-Rho Cross

You may well say "Yes we have found a Chi-Rho cross on the church made up of the statues of St Anthony Hermit, St Roch, and of St Mary Magdalen, St Germaine with an imaginary line the length of the nave to the Altar. We have also seen how Saunière used Constantine's motto on the stoup, but is this Chi-Rho cross just something you have imagined?" No! it is a very important clue to the Cross that we will find later in the Holy Valley of the Cross, but firstly to show how deliberate this is we will study the Chi-Rho cross.

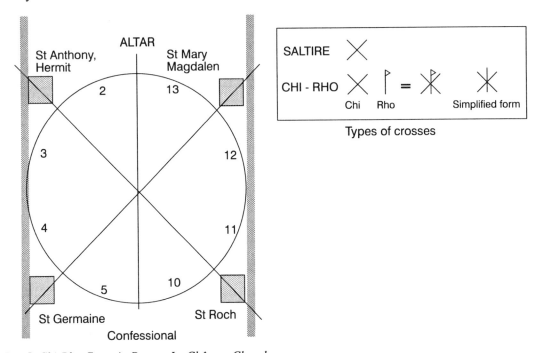

Fig. 5. Chi-Rho Cross in Rennes Le Château Church.

16

This cross was adopted by the early Christians as a monogram for Jesus because the Greek letters Chi (CH) and Rho (R) are the first two letters of CHRISTOS or Christ, in which the capital Chi is written like our letter X, and the Rho like our P. Combined as a monogram we have the P in the middle of the X (our saltire cross). Sometimes this was made with just a plain stroke like an I instead of a P.

The Greek alphabet has 24 letters used to represent the numbers from 1 to 24 in alphabetical order. These traditional values enumerate the 24 cantos of the Iliad and those of the Odyssey, as well as the tablets of the Dodonean oracle priests. Later the Milesian cipher followed the Phoenician/Jewish enumeration.

Rho was the seventeenth letter and therefore 17, and Chi was the twenty second letter and 22. So here it is — St Anthony's day on January the 17th and St Mary Magdalen's on July the 22nd not only forming our saltire × in the church of St Mary Magdalen (× or Chi = 22) but also giving us the Chi-Rho (22 + 17).

There is another interesting thing about the number 22. We have seen how Saunière was fond of the Celtic cross which he often used in varying forms in the decoration of his church. A Celtic cross is a Greek cross in a circle whose arms in both types are all of the same size, this cross is therefore composed of five cubes. Its four arms can be taken to represent the four Cherubim with the heads of a man, ox, lion, and eagle, representing the fixed signs Aquarius, Taurus, Leo, and Aquila (for Scorpio) and the elements air, earth, fire, and water, and the central cube of the cross standing for ether and Spirit. Byzantine religious art was very fond of figuring these Cherubim.

In this cross of five cubes, there are five faces visible in the front and similarly five at the back, making ten in all. On the sides of the cross, there are three exposed on each of the four arms (on one of which it may stand) making twelve faces in total. Each arm can stand for a season of three months of the year, and the twelve faces for the Apostles and also the zodiacal signs. Added together we have 22 faces in all. So now we see how appropriate the 22nd is to St Mary Magdalen. There is a lot more symbolised in this three dimensional cross of which we have seen the key to its revelation, which I will leave the reader to meditate upon; mentioning in passing that the Latin cross represents the opening up of a Cube and is of two dimensions.

Before Our Lord died upon the cross he repeated the first words of Psalm XXII Eloi Eloi Lama Sabachthani 'My God, My God, why hast thou forsaken me?' (Matthew XXVII, v 46, Mark XV, v 34). In this psalm is also mentioned the 'scorning', 'casting of lots for his clothes' etc. Here again is the number 22, which is the 'end' letter of the Hebrew alphabet, the Tau Cross.

Valley of the Cross

With our clues let us now go over to the Valley of the Cross as the valley of Rennes les Bains was known in the 18th century, and which I believe was known as such from the earliest Christian times if not even earlier.

Where is the Cross? and how is it formed? For this surely does not just refer to a wayside cross of which today we have no knowledge. Let us try to find it with our principal clues.

One of the springs at the Source de la Madeleine
(all destroyed by the floods in September 1992).

St Mary Magdalen

We have on the right bank of the river Blanque the Source de la Madeleine. Boudet says that this spring had only recently been known as the Source of the Magdalen, and that on the large scale maps it is called the 'Source de la Gode', named after the hill behind it. Dr Gourdin who wrote the book *Spa of Rennes les Bains* in 1874 informs us that it owes its name to a young girl called Madeleine who used this spring for a cure in 1871, a year before Boudet was installed. Maybe, or is someone trying to put us off the track? Anyhow as we shall see later, the name seems to be most appropriate, not only as it is that of the saint of the church of Rennes le Château, but for other reasons which we will come to.

St Anthony the Hermit

Is there any reason to think that Anthony could be connected with our valley as the only church dedicated to him in the region is at Espéraza?

18

On the upper reaches of the River Blanque, approximately south-east of our valley, is the village of Bugarach, which had an ancient traditional festival held on Ash Wednesday in which a Hermit carried a cross on the centre of which was hung a horse collar with its bells, and on the arms of the cross were hung some sausages.

The cross here seems to indicate our Valley of the Cross below Bugarach, and the horse-collar the pagan solar circle, our Cromleck, for the horse was sacred to Apollo. St Anthony the Hermit, the most renowned one of the Church, is normally depicted with a staff, bell, and pig, as his attributes, so why the horse collar and sausages?

On St Anthony's day horses are blest at Rome, and on the same day the pagans sacrificed swine to the Earth goddess, hence the pig is associated with St Anthony and doubtless in this case the sausages were made of pork. Thus this ancient festival seems to preserve the memory of the cross in our Valley for which we are looking.

The Hermitage

A little further up stream from the Source of the Madeleine a Hermitage is marked on the map, this is situated just below the road and near the river, and consists of a large overhanging rock against which, a brick wall was built to provide a shelter. It is claimed that this was built by a retired soldier of the First Empire, called the Grognard, but whose real name we do not know. (At the beginning of the 19th century, the term Grognard or 'Grumbler' was often applied to veteran soldiers especially of the Napoleonic wars.) Being a talented gardener he cultivated the ground around his cave which he turned into a most picturesque garden which was often visited by strangers staying at Rennes les Bains for the cure. It is asserted that this was the origin of the so called Hermitage, but this is unlikely, for it would not have been possible for him to have settled here, being a stranger and a person with obviously little money, even though it was common ground, unless the shelter under the rock had already been in existence and used in the past as a hermitage. Doubtless it originally had a dry wall of stones around it, which he improved with brick walling. Now as St Anthony is the chief Hermit of the Church, we can associate the Hermitage with him, St Anthony like all true monks and hermits had to overcome the terrible temptations of the devil, by often making the sign of the cross.

We have now found the meaning of two of the clues that Saunière has left us. St Anthony refers to the Hermitage, and the masculine or vertical axis of the Cross, and the feminine and horizontal axis is marked by the Source of the Madeleine of St Mary Magdalen. This however is not sufficient to lay out the Cross, we need at least another marker, but where?

The Devil's Chair

Just south of the circle above the left bank of the River Sals, we climb up to the Fauteuil du Diable (the Devil's Armchair) with the little spring of the Circle alongside. It can be compared to the rocks in the British Isles known as King Arthur's Chairs, or Thrones of the Arch Druids, which being of pagan origin are often referred to as belonging to the Devil.

Often one finds a rock called the Chair with a spring alongside. For example, on the Isle of Man there is such a rock and spring named after St Maughold that delineates the beginning of the South side half of the island, similarly the North side begins with another rock and a

Sitting on the Roche Tremblante.

The Devil's armchair.

20

spring called the Chair of St Patrick. Thus the island was divided into two kingdoms by the pagan Celts, and these ancient markers have been renamed after the first Christian missionaries connected with it.

The carved stone called the Armchair of the Devil resembles the Cathedra called the Throne of St Vigor in the church of Bayeux, which tradition claims dates from his time in the first half of the 6th century, which (as we will find out later) is the period of our Cross.

Some have claimed that our Chair is a modern fake of the last century, but even if it were so it would not alter the fact that a rock may have been known by this name at the same spot since pagan times.

Cathedra

Like the throne of a king, a bishop has as the seat of his authority his chair or Cathedra in the principal church of his diocese, and all the bishops in the early Christian Church were called Papas, or Fathers of their people. When the Bishop of Rome aspired to control all the Christians and became head of the Latin Church in the lands controlled by the Roman Empire, they called him the Papa of Rome, and henceforth the Pope. The Celtic Church in Gaul and elsewhere resented this self imposed authority of the Papa of Rome, and it was only because of the conquest of the Franks who were recent converts to Christianity that he was able to force the south of France to submit; nevertheless this spirit of independence, long after the struggles of the Celtic Church with Rome were forgotten, continued, sometimes appearing overtly as in the case of the Cathars, the Huguenots, and other Protestants. Doubtless the Cathedra of the Pope of Rome was by many called the Devil's Chair. This Chair at Rome which is claimed to have been used by St Peter, has a festival day of its own, it is held on the 18th of January the morrow of St Anthony's fête.

We see that Saunière put the statue of St Anthony Hermit next to the pulpit (in French Chaire which means a pulpit, throne, seat, or chair). So here we have a third marker of the Cross, the Fauteuil du Diable.

The Cross

We now have the vertical axis of our Cross which we have searched for, it passes through the Hermitage and the Devil's Armchair.

The Source of the Madeleine

The horizontal axis passes from the Source of the Madeleine at right angles of course to the vertical axis to somewhere in the west on what is called the Homme Mort or Dead Man, to the east of the Source of the Madeleine one can extend the arm of the Cross to pass through the Fontaine des Amours, Fountain of the Loves, beside the River Sals. This is most appropriate as Mary Magdalen was famed for her many lovers before coming nearer to Jesus (or the centre of our Cross) through her conversion and penitence. Her salvation and ours is attained through the sacrificial death of Christ upon the Cross. It is therefore appropriate

21

that the western arm of the Cross falls on the Homme Mort, where the sun also sets or 'dies' daily in the west.

In the past there were less trees and more pasturage in the Valley, which would apply to the Homme Mort. For this reason Saunière probably chose the shepherdess St Germaine to represent this arm of the Cross, and as we saw he put her opposite St Mary Magdalen in our saltire cross.

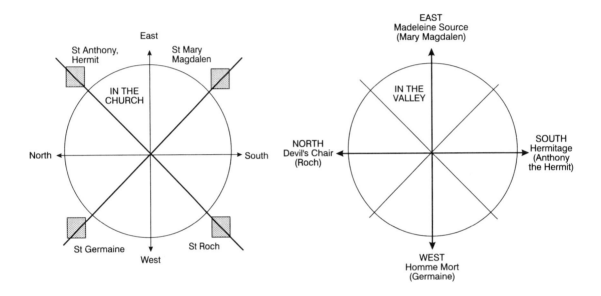

Fig. 6. The crosses in the church and Valley.

Saltire Cross

Let us compare this cross in the church with the cross in the Valley. The Saltire cross is oriented North-East to South-West and South-East to North-West, whilst our Cross in the Valley is to the cardinal points. St Anthony, who is next to the pulpit in the North-East, clearly belongs to the Hermitage in the southern arm of the Cross in the Valley, we can thus put St Roch in the north at the Devil's Armchair. We have identified the Devil's Chair with the Chair of St Peter, and have already seen how Peter is the translation of the Aramaic Cephas a Rock, aptly St Roch's name comes from the low Latin Rocca, a rock or boulder.

Nearby, and south of the Devil's Chair we have the Roche Tremblante, the Trembling Rock, a rocking stone which is nearly in line with the vertical axis of the Cross. This has been marked with a Celtic cross, and I found that if one climbs on to it one can make it rock slightly, but was informed by a local person that it moved much more easily in the past.

22

In the above diagram of the Valley Cross we can exclude the date of St Roch's festival as this here is that of St Peter's Chair, and also that of St Germaine of Pibrac a modern saint, noting however that the summer solstice falls in her octave. It was however on the morrow of St Germaine's day, the 16th of June that the French nun Marguerite Marie Alacoque (1647-1690) had the vision which led to her founding the devotion to the Sacred Heart of Jesus. She was born on the 22nd of July, and after being blessed in 1864 was canonised in 1920. It is interesting to note that the Comte de Chambord gave a large sum towards the building of the basilica of the Sacré Coeur in Paris, and his widow gave a small gift to Saunière.

The Devil in Rennes le Château Church.

II   The Druidic Year

In the Cross that we have found in the Valley we see that we have the festivals of St Mary Magdalen on the 22nd of July and St Anthony and St Peter's Chair on the 17th and 18th of January respectively. What is the significance of these dates? The day of St Anthony is nearly opposite that of St Mary Magdalen for we find that:

There are 180 days from July 22nd to January 17th inclusive, and 185 days from January 18th to July 21st inclusive. It would appear that we have here a calendar similar to that of the Ancient Egyptian Wandering Year which had twelve months of thirty days each, and five Intercalary days "Which do not belong to the year" (i.e. the original year of 360 days). The cycle started with the observation of the heliacal rising of Sothis (Sirius), and probably at a much earlier period, from that of Spica in Virgo. Sirius at the latitude of Memphis rose just before the sun on thc 20th of July (Julian) each year. Because the Wandering Year was about a quarter of a day short of the true year it gained over it and therefore its months travelled all around the calendar of the Tropical year, and did not correspond to its seasons.

After 1,461 wandering years it again agreed with the year marked by the heliacal rising of Sirius, that is after 1,460 Sothic years. It was found necessary to have a more exact calendar, in order to agree with the seasons based on the heliacal rising of Sothis, thus called the Sothic year, in which the adjustment was made to the wandering year by the addition of an extra Intercalary day every fourth year.

This calendar after many thousand years of use in Egypt was adopted by Julius Caesar, whose only change to it was to start the Julian year in winter, and at this time the rising of Sirius took place on the 20th of July. In our case it is here on the 22nd, as they have probably taken the heliacal rising of Sirius for the latitude of Jerusalem.

Amongst the Ancient Egyptians Sothis was personified as a goddess who was associated both with the goddess Isis and also the goddess Hathor. Isis with her desert dog god Anubis the jackal wandered all over Egypt looking for the pieces of her murdered husband the god Osiris, likewise, in the Heavens, the festival of the heliacal rising of Sothis (Sirius) in the Large Dog (Canis Major) as Anubis, roamed all around the Wandering Year.

The cow goddess Hathor, who was closely united to Isis and consequently taken to be Sothis, was the patron of precious ointments. Isis with her divine child Horus on her lap came to used by the early Christians as the image of the Virgin Mary and the infant Jesus.

Similarly we see that Mary Magdalen who was closely associated with the Virgin Mary at the crucifixion and in her legendary journey to Gaul, has like Hathor been connected with precious ointments for was it not she who anointed the feet of Jesus and dried them with her hair? To Mary Magdalen has been given the opening of the half of our year that coincides with the heliacal rising of Sothis (Sirius).

Two Halves of the Year

The Ancient Egyptian Calendar seems also to have divided the year into two halves, for in the Coptic Calendar (which seems to record most of the agricultural entries of the ancient calendar) we have:

- Bashans 9th (in 1900, May 17th Gregorian). 'Opening of the season of navigation by sea' (Mediterranean).
- Hatur 19th (in 1900 our November 28th) 'Avoid voyaging in the Mediterranean'.

Ignoring the Intercalary days which being a later addition were not considered as part of the year, these dates are ten days out of exactly dividing the year in two. I think this is easily explained by the fact that in the 16th century the Julian Year was ten days ahead of the true solar year, the Latins then corrected this by adopting the Gregorian reckoning. I assume that as this day of opening the navigation season is important it was then amended in the Coptic Calendar, but the close being less so was not, for instance the days of the equinoxes when 'Day and Night are equal' have been corrected up till the present century. Why then not the sailing date above? I think that from the end of the 16th century there had been such an improvement in sailing boats that could ride the storms so these dates were no longer strictly observed, thus originally the 'Opening' would have been on the 19th of Bashans and the 'Close' on the 19th of Hatur, exactly dividing the Coptic year into two halves.

These days seem also to have been associated with the two principal festivals of Osiris, which Plutarch mentions, the death or 'Loss of Osiris' on the 17th of Hathor (Coptic Hatur) which lasted for four days, and the 'Finding of Osiris' on the 19th of Pakhons (Coptic Bashans), which in Plutarch's time was the middle of November and of May. The former being the time when the cold weather began, and the latter the hot, in fact the Coptic calendar has the entry 18th of Bashans 'Beginning of the hot season', thus dividing their year into the winter and summer halves. The former was also connected with the sowing of wheat in Lower Egypt and the latter with its harvest.

In ancient Egypt Pakhons was dedicated to Khensu the moon god (a form of Thoth) whose name meant the 'Traveller' as he crossed the night sky in the form of the moon; Hathor, the goddess of the month named after her, means 'the Abode of Horus', who was the god of the sky personified and solar. Both were amongst the earliest gods of Egypt, and their months here aptly divide the year.

At one time the Greeks also reckoned the sailing season by the dawn rising of the Pleiades in May when it opened and their dusk setting in November at its close. In the Christian era we have the division of the year into two parts by St John the Baptist's birthday in June and that of Jesus in December. This was based on an early tradition of dividing the year by the solstices, or more accurately three days afterwards. The sun is lowest on the meridian at the winter solstice but after three days it is seen to climb again into the heavens, and is figuratively 'born', it then goes on climbing to its highest at the summer solstice, but three days later it is perceived to fall and continues thus till the next winter solstice.

This was compared to the lunar month which from the appearance of the new crescent moon waxed for half the month to its glory at its full, and then waned until it disappeared completely from the night sky.

As the moon's month is divided by its phases of waxing and waning, so the year also seemed to be divided by the solstices when the sun rose and waxed stronger in the heavens and then waned as it fell and weakened as we have seen. The moon is just the opposite to the sun, being at its lowest in the sky at the summer solstice, to be born three days afterwards when it begins to rise again in the sky, and reaching its highest at the winter solstice.

Now the moon, because of the morning dew and its cool light, was associated with the element water, and likewise the sun, because of its heat, with that of fire. St John the Baptist was naturally connected with the moon, and Jesus with the baptism of fire and the Holy Spirit therefore with the sun. John was considered by Christians as the forerunner of Christ, so the moon's half of the year up to his birth, (i.e. from St John's day[*] on the 25th of June when the moon is 'born' until the winter solstice when it reaches its highest) belonged to him. Similarly, from the 25th of December when the sun is born, until it reaches its summit, was the half of Jesus. Now the birth of Christ symbolises the beginning of the Christian era, whilst St John stood for the forerunner at the end of the old, hence the remark attributed to St John the Baptist 'He must increase but I must decrease' (John III.30).

Celtic Year

The Celtic year was originally also divided into two halves beginning with the Samhain Fair (November 1st) and the second half with the Beltain Fair (May 1st), later it was quartered into four seasons by the Fairs of Oimelc (February 1st) and Lugnasad (August 1st).

Sothic Year

The ancient Egyptian Sothic year was tied to the heliacal rising of Sirius (20th of July) because it was observed that this regularly happened just before the rise of the Nile on which Egyptian agriculture depended, also at this hot time of year there were few agricultural activities, so it was a suitable period for festivities.

In Europe however the converse is the case, so in this event if they had adopted the Egyptian correction to the 360 day year before the Julian Year, one would expect to find the Intercalary festive days in the beginning of January. In our case we would have:

Intercalary days	18th to the 22nd of January
First half of the year	23rd January to 21st of July
Second half of the year	22nd July to the 17th of January

Which is exactly what the memorial dates of the Chair of St Peter, St Anthony and St Mary Magdalen imply.

---

[*]   Instituted in 448 AD, but in the East and in Gaul it was held soon after the celebration of the Baptism of Christ at Epiphany. This gives support to the idea that the Celtic Church knew the tradition of the Drudic Year, for here he would represent the last moon of his half, "pouring out its water" as it waned, on the newly born sun god.

The Five Intercalary Days

In this year the five Intercalary days and their saints, to which I have added the planetary rulers of the elements and the appropriate day would be:

Five Intercalary Days				
Date	Saint	Ruler	Day	Element
18th January	Chair of St Peter at Rome. SS. Paul and 36 companions in Egypt.	Jupiter ♃	Thursday	Water
19th January	St Germanicus 161 AD. St Bassian bishop of Lodi, about 409 AD	Venus ♀	Friday	Air
20th January	St Fabian, pope, martyr 236 AD. St Sebastian, martyr 287 AD. The Sun enters Aquarius, day of house of Saturn.	Saturn ♄	Saturday	Earth
21st January	St Agnes martyr 306 AD.	Mars ♂	Tuesday	Fire
22nd January	St Vincent martyr 303 AD.	Mercury ☿	Wednesday	Ether

It would appear that the planets were given to these days, and that this year may originally have consisted of 73 five day weeks. The Sunday and Monday of the sun and moon arc naturally excluded in a five Day week, which is similar to the Egyptian 36 Decans and five Intercalary days.

18th January Chair of St Peter

The first day of the ancient Egyptian Intercalary Days was the birthday of Osiris who the Romans likened to Jupiter, the former being the river god and the latter the storm and rain god. Here therefore is the element Water.

Osiris was considered chief of one of the groups of Egyptian gods and Jupiter as chief of the Roman ones, similarly St Peter being the chief Apostle was considered as the head of the Christian Church. Osiris was written in Hieroglyphs with the image of a Seat and an Eye, the throne of royalty and the all-seeing eye. St Peter and his successors replaced for the Christians in Rome the Pontifex Maximus of Jupiter and the Roman gods, thus the Chair of St Peter became the seat of authority by which the bishops of Rome claimed not only to be the papa of this city, but also over the whole Christian Church.

As we have already seen, Peter's name meant a Rock, and this was also the symbol of Jupiter, for when his father Saturn tried to swallow all his children the other gods, in order to get rid of them, a rock was substituted for Jupiter which made him vomit and bring them all back again. Jupiter later deposed Saturn and became king of the gods.

St Peter also inherited the keys of the god Janus after which this month of January is named; he was the doorkeeper who was placed between the old and new year which he opened. Peter's seat of authority is therefore very appropriate here at the beginning of the Intercalary Days and the Year and it is interesting to note that the old Chair of St Peter in the Vatican has carved on its front the twelve Labours of Hercules and six signs of the Zodiac.

SS Paul and his 36 companions

In Egypt at a very early but unknown date a group of 37 Christian soldiers decided to propagate the Gospel, they split up into four groups of nine men and their leader Paul went with the first group to the East, whilst the others went to the South, West, and North. The Governor of Egypt being very alarmed at the state of affairs ordered that they should be immediately executed, those who went to the East and South were burnt, those to the west were crucified, and the ones in the North were beheaded. In this story I think that we may have an allegory representing our year, for they were all martyred on the 18th of January, Paul stands for the Intercalary days and his 36 companions the Decans, which here split into four groups for the four seasons.

Burning in the East, and the Spring

Here we have the burning up of the stars at sunrise, and especially the burnt offering of lambs and Aries at the vernal equinox.

Burning in the South, and Summer

The heat of the midday sun when it crosses the meridian, particularly in midsummer.

Crucifixion in the West, and Autumn

The sun dies daily, and also the moon and stars in the West; and the sun is crucified at the autumn equinox when it crosses to below the equator, when the days grow shorter.

Beheading in the North, and Winter

The moon is at its highest on the meridian at the winter solstice, and is 'beheaded' like St John the Baptist, and rolls down again, (the Rev Owen tells us that the feast of the Decollation of St John the Baptist on August the 29th is said really to signify the gathering up of his bones or relics). Their leader Paul of course goes to the East where the sun resurrects daily, and especially at the vernal equinox when it crosses to above the equator in the constellation that marks our era, being around the time of Easter and the Resurrection of Jesus after his crucifixion.

28

19th January St Bassian

As a boy he protected a doe with her two fawns from a group of hunters who were in pursuit, he threw his arms around the neck of the beast so that they could not kill it. (Deer because of their swiftness are symbols of the wind).

The planet venus, as we have here no Moon day, stands for all the goddesses, thus aptly we have in the story of St Bassian the deer, which is an animal particularly sacred to Diana the goddess of hunting. The goddess Venus whilst normally associated with the carnal aspect of love, for fertility, also represents its higher form as demonstrated by St Bassian.

The planet venus is connected with the element of Air, which in the Yoga philosophy is allocated to the Heart Chakra because of the lungs on either side.

20th January: St Fabian. Sun enters Aquarius

This is the middle day of the week and is conspicuous by the fact that on this day the sun traditionally enters the Sign of Aquarius, we have here the day house of saturn, and it is an Air sign, thus the story told of Fabian that a dove descended upon his head when he was being balloted for as pope, it was taken as a good omen which decided his election.

This is interesting here for Air is the particular element of birds, and of course the dove is a symbol of the Holy Spirit.

The planet saturn and its ruler are linked to the element of Earth, and the name Saturn is thought to be derived from Sator the Sower or Planter, it was because this planet takes the longest time of the planets known to antiquity to travel around the heavens that it was likened to a slow old man, so the god Saturn was thought to be its ruler, and was the chief of the gods until deposed by his son Jupiter.

Fabian obviously belonged to the Fabia Gens which was one of the oldest patrician families of Rome, thus appropriately agreeing with the main characteristic of Saturn.

Because primitive man buried his dead in the earth, their spirits were believed to go on living in the Underworld of the Great Mother, therefore the earliest gods were chthonic, the element of Saturn. In passing we should mention that Chinese start their lunar year with the full moon in this sign, which may have been originally a solar year like the old Tibetan one that began with the sun entering the constellation of Aquarius.

St Sebastian

We have here St Sebastian who was born locally, at Narbonne, he was martyred by being shot to death with arrows (through the Air). His name resembles Sebasteia the old name of Sivas in Turkey, this may derive from the god Sabazios the Thracian patron of agriculture, similar to Saturn. Later he naturally became the patron saint of soldiers, and as the following day is dedicated to Mars the god of war, this is not altogether inappropriate.

This day belongs to the element Earth and its ruler is Saturn, on this day the sun moves into Aquarius, an Air sign, from Capricorn, an Earth one, both however are ruled by Saturn. Here the Dove of St Fabian and the Arrows of St Sebastian are symbols of Air, nevertheless the presence of Saturn implies the Earth. We have here two Air symbols when we should expect to find those of Earth, this is probably because of the importance of the sun's entry into Aquarius, and of the fact that the Calendar and the Zodiac both belong to the Heavens.

21st January: St Agnes

In the fourth century this Virgin martyr of the Diocletian persecution was the most popular female saint, and it was only after the Council of Ephesus in 431 AD that it was decided to give special reverence to the Virgin Mary. Her name comes from AGNUS, Latin for *lamb* particularly in the sense of a sacrificial animal, on whose day at Rome the 'Blessing of the Lambs' from whose wool the pallium of the Archbishops is made, takes place. Agnus is clearly related to the Sanskrit Agni, or Fire, personified as the god of the sacrificial flame, thus we have IGNIS meaning Fire in Latin, which element belongs to Mars.

Agnus recalls the constellation of Aries the Ram being burnt in the sun's rays at the time of the vernal equinox, and the consequent offering of the newly born lambs, as a pagan 'First Fruits' offering of the lambs which were born at this time of year, originally sacrificed at the 'threshold' of the homes and later on at the temples, here very apt at the Threshold of our Druidic Year.

22nd January: St Vincent

Born at Saragossa in Aragon, he suffered cruel torture particularly by Fire for refusing to sacrifice to the gods. His dead body was cast into a field to become the prey of wild beasts, and birds (hence Air), it was then thrown into the sea (Water), and it was washed up on the shore whence it was buried by the Christians (Earth). The Intercalary day here being Wednesday the day of Mercury and the element Ether which contains and unites all the other elements, which is illustrated by the above story. The planet mercury always appears close to the sun before dawn and after sunset, because of this the god and regent of this planet was thought to be the guide of the young souls about to be born at the 'coming forth', and of the dead at the 'returning to' the Underworld, and also the earliest gods were chthonic and he was their messenger. This concept is the earlier one before the souls were imagined to descend from heaven at the summer solstice, thus Mercury appropriately has his day here at the end of the Intercalary days and the eve of a new Druidic Year.

Pentagram of the Week

Originally the five day week would have started with Saturn's day (Saturday) but as Jupiter had replaced him as king of the gods it starts here with his day (Thursday), if we look at Fig. 8 we see that if we go around the pentagram starting with Jupiter (Thursday), Venus (Friday), Saturn (Saturday), and so on we have the order as in the above Intercalary five day week.

The seven day week just adds in the 'Sun's day and that of the Moon between those of Saturn and Mars, and in the case of our Intercalary days we have even the sun here as it enters the sign of Aquarius on the 20th of January, a Saturday. In the five day week we find the order of the planets by starting with saturn and going through the pentagram, jupiter, mars etc., however, in the seven day week the converse is the case, the order of the planets goes around the Heptagram, and that of the days through it. We will discuss this further when we come to The Pentagram in Ancient Egypt.

23rd January. The First Half of the Year

This day is obviously considered to be important for we have on this day:

- St Parmenas martyr one of the first 7 Deacons.
- St Emerentiana virgin martyr, foster-sister of St Agnes 305 AD
- St John the almsgiver, Patriarch of the holy See of St. Mark and also Patron of the knights of St. John of Jerusalem, the Hospitallers AD 609
- "Memorial of our first parents Adam and Eve" in the British Sarum martyrology

This latter event seems to confirm that it was considered the beginning of an ancient year among the Celtic church. Between the years 1040 - 1050 AD the citizens of Amalfi erected two hospices for the pilgrims of the Latin Rite, near the Church of the Holy Sepulchre, that for men was dedicated to St. John the almsgiver and the other for women to St Mary Magdalen, who are the saints which mark the two halves of our year.

The chapel for the new buildings was first dedicated to St John the almsgiver and later in the beginning of the 12th century rededicated to St John the Baptist, both these St Johns started a half of the year, and one has replaced the other. It throws considerable light on the Masonic problem as to which St John the St John's Lodges, of the old Operative masons, were dedicated.

When Jerusalem fell to the Christians in the first crusade, their leader Godfrey de Bouillon was elected ruler of the Holy City on the 22nd of July 1099; the day of St Mary Magdalen and the beginning of the second half of our year.

Though it would appear that this year could have come down to us either from the last century BC when the cult of Isis had penetrated Europe, or from the early Christian Culdees who came to the British Isles from North Africa in the first centuries AD, nevertheless it appears to be much older, and I think it may really be Megalithic, but let us call it The Druidic Year. If we look for other traces of this year we find:–

Terms.

The law courts in England and Scotland sit for four periods in the year which are called the Terms, which word originates from Terminus the Roman god of boundaries and landmarks, though this is not their original Celtic name and cannot therefore be taken as a guide to their origin. In Scotland they are obviously older.

In England the first and last were fixed, but the middle two Terms were variable being tied to Easter (the dates were changed later by Act of Parliament in 1831).

Thus we see that both of these sets of Terms originally started their first Term on the 23rd of January, and the Scottish Lammas Term starts on the 20th of July, the time of the heliacal rising of Sirius at Memphis of the Sothic Calendar at the beginning of the Christian Era. The old Celtic year started with Samhain on the 1st of November, this became the Christian All Saint's Day; followed on the 2nd by All Soul's Day. It is therefore clear that these Terms originally started with the Celtic Year, as the Term of Martinmas in Scotland begins on the 3rd of November following All Souls Day, whilst that of Michaelmas in England had apparently been moved to three days later.

Scottish Terms		
Candlemas Term	23 January to 12 February	21 days
Whitsuntide Term	25 May to 15 June	22 days
Lammas Term	20 July to 8 August	20 days
Martinmas Term	3 November to 29 November	27 days
	Total	90 days
English Terms		
Hilary Term	23 January to 12 February	21 days
Easter Term	Wednesday fortnight after Easter day to the first Monday after Ascension Day	27 days
Trinity Term	Friday following Trinity Sunday to Wednesday fortnight	20 days
Michaelmas Term	6 November to 28 of November	23 days
	Total	91 days

The interesting question arises as to why was January 18th given to the Cathedra of St Peter at Rome? It was originally kept on the 22nd of February (Depositio Martyrdom 354 AD) on which day St Austin informs us that Peter received the chair of the episcopate. However, it was probably the date of his martyrdom because it was so called in a very ancient calendar (the Deposition of St Peter and St Paul). This festival reached Gaul by the time of the Calendar of Polemus Silvius (448 AD) and that of Tours (490 AD). Later the date was changed and in the Hieran Martyrdom in Gaul the Gallican editor noted two dates, that of the Chair of St Peter at Rome January 18th, and he called the older date the Chair of St Peter at Antioch, even though this festival had never been introduced into the East ! This seems to indicate that our year belonged to the Celtic Church and may even date from Pagan times.

In addition to what we have already noted, there is the fact that July in Wales was called Gorphenhav which means the 'End of summer or the year' and Pliny (Nat: Hist: LXVI c.44) writing in the first century states that the Celtic year began in July.

Pied Piper

In Brunswick the story of the Pied Piper of Hameln whose day is the 22nd of July may be based on our year. He piped and drew away the plague of rats (or the long dark nights of winter and the first half of the year?) The stars of Aquarius in which the Chinese year begins, are also those of the Rat, one of the twelve animals after whom their zodiacal signs are named.

When the officers of the town refused to pay him, he piped and drew away all the children after him (or the long days of summer in the second half of the year?). They disappeared into a cave in a mountain. (which resembles the mythical cave or grotto of the period of the winter solstice.) Doubtless it was on the 22nd of July that the children left in the year 1376 (note $1+3+7+6 = 17$) by occult arithmetic, again giving us the number of completion).

Another account gives the date as 1284, and the day that the children were 'piped away' as the 26th of June the feast of S.S. John and Paul, this again points to the year as divided by the two St Johns.

Order of the Garter

One of the most noble institutions of Chivalry the 'Order of the Garter', previously restricted to noble knights, is generally supposed to have been founded on Monday the 19th of January 1344 by King Edward III of England, being the second of our Intercalary days. Obviously it was not inaugurated on the 18th as it was a Sunday.

Calendar of Reason

The Coptic calendar seems to have been used as the basis of the Calendar of Reason which was instituted after the French Revolution, and the months' names appear to have been modelled upon the ancient Gaulish months, which were still preserved in the Dutch almanac of that period. There were thirty days in each month and an extra five Intercalary days which were public holidays corresponding to the 17th to the 21st of September in the Gregorian calendar. The first month of the year called Vindemaire (Vintage) started on the day of the autumnal equinox.

This year was adopted in 1794 when the 17th of September Gregorian fell on Wednesday, sacred to Mercury and his Gallic equivalent Ogham, who as god of the alphabet and writing, like the Egyptian god Thoth, may have been judged appropriate for the first of the five holidays. Here is our number seventeen again, of Osiris on whom the Masonic legend of the murder of Hiram Abiff the architect of King Solomon's temple appears to be based.

The kings of France were thought to have very 'holy blood', presumably because of their coronation rites, connected in a mystical way with that of Jesus, so it was a heinous thing to shed the blood of the king, despite this King Louis XVI was guillotined on Wednesday the 21st of January 1789. This was the fourth Intercalary day of our Druidic Year, the day of St Agnes, the blessing of whose lambs recalls to mind 'the Lamb of God that taketh away the sins of the world', our Paschal Lamb, Jesus. The Cathars of Montségur also went forth to be burnt alive on the eve of their fourth Intercalary day, as we have seen. Did the makers of the Calendar of Reason have some traditional knowledge of our Druidic Year? If this were so, they might think that this bloody deed taking place 'outside the year' would, in some way absolve them from this terrible act.

17th of January and Alchemy

Nicolas Flamel tells us in his book that whilst he was learning about the alchemical process he travelled on a pilgrimage to the shrine of St James the Elder at Compostella, who is the Patron of alchemists and of all cosmological arts and sciences.

His wife Perrenelle with whom he was later to do all his alchemical experiments, was also devoted to St John the brother of St James, these two apostles were called Boanerges or Sons of Thunder (Luke IX 54) probably because of their Heavenly and fiery zeal, which is not without some significance.

He relates that after 21 years he perfected his first alchemical transmutation of mercury into fine Silver "on the 17th of January 1382, a Monday, around midday in my house, with only Perrenelle present", although this day in that year was actually a Friday.

Now Monday and silver are sacred to the Moon, but Friday and copper to Venus, similarly Sunday and gold are sacred to the Sun and Tuesday and iron to Mars, also the Sun is symbolic of the Spirit and the moon of the Soul, whilst Mars represents the male hero striving with matter, and Venus the heroine struggling with the instincts of Nature.

Where he calls Friday a Monday, it may well be in an attempt to bring our attention to this calendrical error, having transmuted a base metal like copper into fine Silver he therefore calls it a Monday. But why the 17th of January? Well St Anthony was a hermit who overcame all the temptations of Nature symbolised by his 'pig', and more relevant still he ends the second half of the Druidic Year, which begins with the day of St Mary Magdalen, as we know, on the 22nd of July, and the 25th is the festival of St James the Elder.

Flamel, began with his pilgrimage to Compostella and finished the work in his own house in Paris, he had done the 'external' work, wandering in search of that which he was to find 'internally' at home with his wife, thus at the end of the Druidic Year he succeeded in the transmutation. Surely he knew all about this Druidic Year.

During this alchemical labour Nicolas represents Mars and Perrenelle Venus, whilst on the completion of the Great Work, he stands for the Sun, gold and Spirit; and she for the Moon, silver and Soul.

We are told that "again in the sole company of Perrenelle in the same house on the 25th day of April of the same year at five o'clock in evening" they transmuted quicksilver into fine Gold. This is the day of St Mark the Evangelist which falls in the zodiacal sign of that beast of burden Taurus the Bull, but he is also associated with the cherub of the Lion, the sign Leo, house of the Sun and gold.

Note Perrenelle as Venus was always present in these operations as we see that:

- 25th of July St James 1381 was a Friday.
- 17th of January St Anthony 1381 was a Friday.
- 25th of April St Mark 1381 was a Friday.

First she was the symbol of the Soul purified, and the base metal such as copper changed into fine Silver, and then he was the symbol of Spirit perfected, iron changed into fine Gold, but one ought to bear in mind that they were united in one house.

The Merovingians

It is interesting to recall here that Dagobert II the last Merovingian king was murdered in the forest of Woevre on Sunday the 23rd of January 679 AD, also according to the chronology of Mezeray, Dagobert I died on the 17th of January 638 AD (note 6+3+8 =I7), though that of Bellefrost states that it was in 645 AD and that his son Clovis II died on the 17th year of his reign.

34

The Planetary Houses of the Zodiac

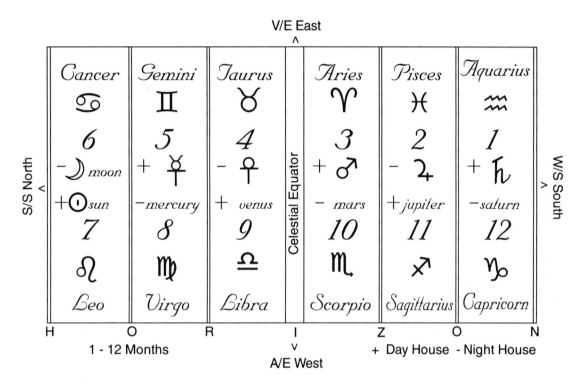

Fig. 7. Planetary Houses.

In the diagram (Fig. 7) I have placed the planets in their traditional order in the Zodiacal houses of Astrology, each planet is put in a division with its day and night house, from saturn to mercury, and the sun and moon which have only one house each are put in Leo and Cancer respectively.

It is most important to remember that unlike the actual constellations, the houses of Astrology which are named after them are divided into twelve equal sections of the Zodiac. It will be seen in the diagram that the houses all fall within seven vertical lines that could have been posts or stones as markers, and this could be placed on either the eastern or western horizon. The furthest to the North would mark the sun rise or set at the Summer Solstice, and conversely that in the South the Winter Solstice, and the middle post would be due East or West and that of the Equinoxes.

From this arrangement we see that the Aries Era is just about to start with the place of the Vernal Equinox between the houses of Taurus and Aries, which happened amongst the constellations around 1,800 BC, nevertheless this arrangement of the planets in their mansions was most likely devised later by the Greeks at the end of the Aries Era.

Our Druidic Year has the sun entering the Sign of Aquarius in the middle of the Intercalary days, which if taken to be originally the place of the winter solstice, claims to date it to the beginning of the Aries Era as in this arrangement.

Age of the Constellations

From the star lists of Aratus, Ptolemy, and others, we find a great gap in the heavens in which no stars and their constellations are given because they could not be seen when these lists were drawn up. As the south pole of the sky has shifted because of the precession of the equinoxes, one can calculate this date, similarly the latitude affects how many stars can be seen. E W Maunder and other astronomers have done so, and one of the latest and most precise is by Dr M W Ovenden who after having gone deeply into the matter came to the conclusion that this happened around 2,600 BC at a latitude of 36° North. He claimed that the sky was probably mapped by a seafaring people and suggested that they lived on Crete, however this could also apply to Malta, whose megalithic monuments are of a very early date and whose builders were skilled in astronomy.

Druidic Year

Perhaps I should have called this the Megalithic year, and I avoided the use of the word Aquarian as this might lead to confusion with the Aquarian Age. (The Druids however are though to have inherited their knowledge from pre-Celtic times.) We have seen that the date of the festival of St Peter's Chair was changed to the 18th of January which enabled it to take the place of importance as the first of the Intercalary Days.

The first day of this year was the 23rd of January which in the British Sarum martyrology is dedicated to the "Memorial of our first parents Adam and Eve", also the feast day of St John of Jerusalem, Patriarch of the holy See of St Mark at Alexandria, and Patron of the knights of St John, the Hospitallers. He died on the 11th of November but this being the day of St Mennas among the Greeks, they remember him on the 12th which is the feast of St Martin among the Latins, the latter allotted to him the 23rd of January, or in other martyrologies the 23rd of February, and the 13th of July. The allocation of the 23rd to St John, the first day of our Druidic Year indicates again its connection with Gaul and Britain.

Hermit of Bugarach

The fact that the Hermit is depicted carrying the Latin Cross with a horse collar and (pork?) sausages hanging from it, I think depicts St Anthony, whose name has been forgotten as the present church is dedicated to the festival of the Assumption which was first instituted in 813 AD. I think we could safely assume that the original church was dedicated to St Anthony the Hermit, and probably existed in Visigothic times because Bugarach's origins are very early, and as Louis Fédié informs us, had been the site of a Gallo Celtic Fort. The first mention of the church that we have is in the Charta of the Lands of the abbey St Polycarpe dating from the end of the 9th century.

With regard to the blessing of Horses at Rome on St Anthony's day it is interesting to note that the heavenly horse Pegasus, is a paranatellon of Aquarius, adjoining it in the North which explains this. Pegasus according to Hesychius comes from the archaic Greek word PEGAS, a pitcher or rock, which explains the Greek fable that when Pegasus kicked the rock water flowed forth to create the fountain of Hippocrene. This fountain was later surrounded by a sacred grove of the Muses, whose water was thought to give inspiration to the poets if

36

Bugarach. (Postcard c. 1920.)

they drank it. This is because the five Intercalary days which are outside our Druidic Year are very magical. Similar is the case of the ancient Egyptian year's Intercalary days, the birthdays of the gods, which the god Thoth won from the Moon god.

Pegasus the moon horse was used for rainmaking. It is therefore likely that the full moon in Aquarius at the summer solstice or around that time, in the era of Taurus, is the origin of this myth, and the big square of Pegasus rising at dusk for a long time afterwards marked the summer solstice.

To this era, as we will see later, belong the legendary King Aquarius and St Saturnin of Toulouse. It is not unlikely that the Gauls of these parts had preserved the memory of the Druidic Year from the megalithic age.

St Anthony has been associated with Tantony or Tan the Celtic fire god, he was still thought of as representing the Spirit of the Hearth among the witches of Etruria in the last century, who were probably perpetuating the remains of the ancient Etruscan religion.

Vesta goddess of the hearth closed the old year, and Janus opened the new one, it is therefore appropriate that we have St Anthony at the end of our Druidic Year.

As the Druids ordered all households to extinguish their fires at the end of the year, and then rekindled the sacred fire for the new year at Samhain (November 1st) which was then carried to every home, so here in our year does not St Anthony represent the time of the renewal of the fire of the hearth?

It is also interesting to recall that in Sardinia, another place of very old traditions, in the Vendetta where a death is to be avenged, they used to do a cursing ceremony for nine days commencing from St Anthony's day.

This covers our magical Intercalary Days, and if this ceremony originally lasted seven days, then that would consist of the last day of the old year, the five Intercalary days, and the first day of the new year.

St Anthony, the hermit of the Egyptian desert, is therefore given the Tau cross which is derived from the Ancient Egyptian Ankh cross, and they both signify Life and not death; to which the Hearth Fire protecting primitive man at night from wild animals, and giving warmth in winter is also appropriate. Similarly the Ankh cross was shown as held by the rays of the sun, the source of life and fertility.

In the ceremony of the Hermit of Bugarach which was held on Ash Wednesday the first day of Lent, he therefore carried the Latin Cross, although the Tau Cross was the attribute of St Anthony, and this day was renowned for the severity of discipline. On this day in the ancient church the Penitents appeared before their Bishops covered only with sack-cloth and with bare feet, to be sprinkled with ashes and submit to whatever punishment should be given to them. Is this one of the reasons that the Rev Saunière had inscribed 'Pénitence Pénitence' upon the pillar?

St Anthony was in his youth a swineherd and his animal is therefore the pig, which indicates the northern arm of our cross in the Valley, falling on the first degree of Sagittarius, the 22nd of November sacred to Diana whose animal was the wild boar. The Gauls had also great esteem for this animal, and they also used the northern orientation for religious purposes. The sausages hanging from the Bugarach's hermit's cross were obviously pork.

Originally horses were lunar, but later solar symbols. Here the horse collar suggests the southern arm of our cross, which marks the 1st degree of Gemini, the 21st of May, sacred to Apollo who as Helios was drawn across the sky in his chariot by four horses.

In connection with our cross we will find two pentagrams as pointed out by Saunière on the pillar, their points fall on all the diferent months of the year, excluding January and July, the two months which divide our Druidic Year, a fact of which the architects of our cross must have been fully aware.

The Hermitage.

Drinking at the Fontaine des Amours.

III   Inner Calendar Alignments

The Zodiac and the Cross.

Placement of the Zodiac

We will now return to the Cross in the Valley. The festival dates of St Mary Magdalen and St Anthony the Hermit do not help us, but it is nevertheless possible to place the zodiacal signs and the year around our Cross. Now in the Pagan beliefs of Europe, rivers, springs and fountains etc. were connected with goddesses, so here at the Source of the Madeleine which has been named after a woman (or the 'young virgin' according to Dr Gourdin) we can place Virgo.

We have seen how in Ancient Egypt the goddess Isis was closely associated with Hathor, these being replaced in Christianity by the Virgin Mary and Mary Magdalen. Both Isis and the Virgin Mary are associated with Virgo, which in the Piscean era was the constellation of the autumnal equinox. So we can place Virgo on the eastern arm of our Cross, at the Source of the Madeleine. Opposite to Virgo is Pisces which goes on the western arm at the Homme Mort.

The sun, moon and stars, are 'born' or rise in the East and 'die' or disappear into the underworld in the West. In the time of Jesus the vernal equinox fell in the end of Pisces, thus the Dead man (Homme Mort) could refer to the crucified Christ.

On the southern arm of the Cross we will place Gemini the constellation of the summer solstice, marked by the Hermitage, and on the northern arm, of the Devil's Chair, that of the winter solstice Sagittarius. From this arrangement we see that the Cross could denote the time of sunrise at the autumn equinox. However, as it falls on the Homme Mort, it is more likely that it stands for the sunset at the vernal equinox, in the Piscean age (and if it falls on Good Friday, the Crucifixion).

There is near Glastonbury in England a large Zodiac which is formed by the shape of the fields. This has the Bull Taurus in the West and the figure depicting Scorpio in the East. This dates that Zodiac for those who accept its legitimacy to the Taurean era, about the same age as the Circles of Avebury and Stonehenge in the neighbouring county. That Field Zodiac, like ours, is laid out in an anticlockwise manner, which is the order of the rising and setting stars as found in the chart of a horoscope.

Dating Our Cross

As we see from the map our cross is not aligned due North and South, but is between 8° and 8°1/2 East of true North. For what reason has it been so oriented? Let us superimpose another cross duly oriented to the cardinal points, with Aries the traditional house of the vernal equinox just about to set in the West. We now see that the western arm of our cross falls about eight and a half degrees into Pisces on the truly oriented cross, and we can reasonably assume that this has been deliberately done to date our cross. Was it then the place of the vernal equinox in Pisces?

The problem now is where did the constellation Aries begin in the heavens? And therefore at what date did the vernal equinoctial point retrogress from the constellation Aries into that of Pisces? It is the same problem which has been much discussed by contemporary Astrologers.

Around 139 BC Hipparchus following his observations, commenced the zodiac with the vernal equinox point falling in the first degree of the constellation Aries. In the lifetime of Jesus we can tell from his choosing the 'fishermen', and brothers or 'twins', for his disciples that he thought the Fish age had just begun, with the vernal equinox at the beginning of the constellation and the sign of Pisces and the summer solstice at the beginning of the sign of Gemini. This is also borne out by the earliest Christians choosing a 'fish' as their emblem.

Nevertheless when we come to Ptolemy the Alexandrian astronomer whose observations were made between 127 and 151 AD, he still showed the vernal equinoctial point as in the first degree of Aries! Similarly this is still kept as the vernal equinoctial point though it bears no relationship to the constellation after which it is named.

Why should Ptolemy and Hipparchus agree about the equinoctial point when about 270 years separated them, and because of the precession of the equinox it had retrograded through about 3° to 4° on the ecliptic? The answer is clearly that the important cosmic myth of the 'sacrificial lamb of God' relating to the sun entering the Ram (Aries) at the vernal equinox and it being 'burnt up' in the rays of the sun, and all other similar myths of that era would otherwise be false. Everything similar relating the constellations to the calendar, that was built into the mythology of Religion and the Astrological system, and the teaching of the Mystery Schools, would have to be changed for the era of the 'Fishes of God'.

The long established traditions had become crystallised, and the real esoteric meanings were mostly forgotten having been kept secret too long by the elite, and the exoteric explanations degenerated into mere superstitions. It was more than Hipparchus and Ptolemy dared to admit that the vernal equinox now fell in Pisces, so they kept on extending the beginning of the constellation Aries. Whilst at the beginning the Christians adopted the symbol of the Fish for Christ the Lord of the new religion and era, they dropped this in the 3rd century and adopted the more discreet Vesica Piscis symbol. As the equinoctial point moved further into the constellation of Pisces, in order to save the traditional system of Astrology, the vernal equinoctial point was taken to mark the beginning of the sign of Aries. The Zodiac was divided into 12 equal signs having the same names even though they had ceased to correspond to their constellations and stars.

The Date

If one takes the statement of Hipparchus about the spring equinox falling at the beginning of the constellation Aries (a fact likely to be known to the originators of our cross), then 8° to 8°1/2 into Pisces gives us 575 - 608$^{1}/_{2}$ years of precession. As Hipparchus observed this in 139 BC, this dates our cross to between 435 and 470 AD, but more precisely I reckon this to be around 448 AD.

The observations of Ptolemy in 127 AD at the earliest would give us 700 AD which is too late. Alternatively, though I think it is also too late, our 8° - 8$^{1}/_{2}$° into the constellation Pisces could be taken to date from the beginning of the Christian Era. This was devised by Dionysius Exiguus who took the year of the Annunciation as 1 AD, he persuaded Justinian to substitute it for the old Roman reckoning throughout the Empire in 523 AD, and by 730 AD it prevailed in the West. This 8° - 8½° of precession, would give us 573 - 609 AD, (and falling in the reign of the Visigothic King Reccared (586 - 604) who abjured Arianism). It would help to account for the wide range of saints that we will discover to be connected with the alignments of our Cross, though many were evidentially added later.

If, as is quite possible, those who laid out the Cross had not used an astronomical observation of the point of the vernal equinox but reckoned it from the date, then as they thought 1° of precession took 72 years (rather than the modern 71.6 years) we should add about 3 years to the above calculations. I think our cross may have been inspired by Galla Placidia (who died in 450 AD), who we will discuss later.

The Alignments and the Calendar

As the Valley Cross symbolises the Piscean Era of Christianity, I think we should put the signs of the zodiac around our cross with Pisces instead of Aries about to set in the West, and similarly Virgo instead of Libra in the East. We have Pisces and the crucified Jesus, or Dead Man (Homme Mort) in the West, and Virgo or the Virgin Mary in the east at the source of the Madeleine. We can identify Madeleine (Mary Magdalen) with Virgo as well as Mary to whom she served as a companion on their journey to Gaul, just as the goddesses Hathor and Isis were both identified with Sothis.

I drew up a list of most of the springs, ruins and prominent peaks etc. to be found around our Cross, and the angle in degrees which each alignment makes from the centre of the Cross and the beginning of Pisces. (Not the end, as it has taken the place of the sign of Aries.) This is measured anti-clockwise as shown in a horoscope, which is the way that the constellations are seen to follow each other in the night sky. Then I have shown the corresponding date in the Calendar with the saint commemorated, and also some Old Testament personalities, and Pagan gods, etc.

There is however one problem in the fact that whilst the northern and southern axis of our cross is well defined by the Devil's Chair and the Hermitage, that of the horizontal one is not so clear. There is no precise marker in the valley of the Homme Mort, and it is not certain that the eastern arm which goes to the Source of the Madeleine also passes through the Fontaine des Amours, but I have taken this to be the case. The slightest variation however changes the position of the centre of the cross and consequently affects the angle of the alignments and their Calendar dates; also some of the Ruins may be comparatively modern, though probably built on the sites of earlier buildings, so little is known about them.

I have tried to keep to saints who lived before 470 AD when our Cross may have been laid out, though I think others were added later where appropriate in the Visigothic period, and new farms built to serve as markers, but now in ruins, certain springs may also have been embellished for the same purpose. It is clear from some later and locally important saints that the Merovingians also knew all about our Cross as we shall see. It would appear, for example, that the alignment to the church of Rennes le Château which falls on the day of St Bathilde Queen of France and wife of King Clovis II, the son of Dagobert I, who died in 680 AD seems to imply that her day has been deliberately chosen so that the original church on the site of St Mary Magdalen commemorated the royal saint.

42

		Inner Alignments Around the Cross		
Degree	Location	Date	Event	AD
81/2° +	La Pique	27 Feb. 28 Feb.	— 'The finding of the child Jesus in the Temple'.	
2nd ☆ 22°	Fontaine Valdieu Les Boudous ruins	(12 Mar. (12 Mar. 13 Mar.	St Paul Aurelian, bishop.) St Gregory, pope.) St Eupraxia, virgin.	573 604 410
261/2°	Fontaine des Quatre Ritous	17 Mar. 18 Mar.	St Patrick. St Gabriel, Archangel.	464
341/2° 4th ☆	Serre Mijane ruin	25 Mar. 26 Mar.	'Annunciation of the BVM.' Dismas the good thief who hung on the cross on the right side of Jesus. —	
371/2° 4th ☆	Ruin at bottom of Pas de la Roque	28 Mar. 29 Mar.	St Gontran, king, grandson of Clovis and St Clotilde. —	525 - 593
451/2°	Les Gavignauds ruins	5 Apr. 6 Apr.	St Irene, virgin, martyr. St Marcellinus, martyr.	c.290 413
491/2° 1st ☆	La Jasse du Bézu	9 Apr. 10 Apr.	St Mary Cleophas. Ezekiel, prophet.	
511/2° 1st ☆	le Bézu Church	11 Apr. 12 Apr.	St Antipas 'the faithful witness', bishop. St Leo the great, pope, resisted the Huns. St Sabas the Goth, martyr	180 461 372
68°MC 3rd ☆	La Jacotte ruins	28 Apr.	St Vitalis, martyr, patron of Ravenna.	62
801/2° MC	Les Baruteaux ruin	11 May 12 May	St Mamertus, bishop of Vienne. St Epiphanius, bishop.	477 403
90° 2nd ☆ MC C	L'Ermitage	21 May	Apollo, god. Emperor Constantine. St Hospitius, hermit at Nice.	272 - 337 580
99° +	La Ferrière Source ■	30 May	Death of King Arthur fighting the Saxons, who bore a cross and picture of the BVM on his shield.	6th C
1081/2° 4th ☆	Vialasse Source ■ and Mine Ruins	8 Jun. 9 Jun.	St Medard bishop of Noyen, patron of vineyards and St Gildard bishop of Rouen, twins St Columba of Iona, abbot.	 545 597
1231/2° 1st ☆	Vialasse ruin to the East	24 Jun. 25 Jun.	Midsummer's day. St John the Baptist. Pontius Pilate in the Coptic Church, it asserts he died a Christian. St Prosper of Aquitaine, Church father.	 457
134°	El Casteil ruin	6 Jul.	Isiah, prophet.	
139°HD 3rd ☆	Bugarach Church	12 Jul.	St Hermagoras, disciple of St Mark, martyr, the first bishop of Aquileia.	

Degree	Location	Date	Event	AD
159° 2nd ✭ MC	La Pourteille ruins	1 Aug. (2 Aug. (3 Aug.	Lugnasad. Lammas. St Peter in chains. St Stephen, pope, martyr.) Invention of St Stephen.)	257 415)
164° 2nd ✭	Source near les Carbounières	6 Aug.	St Sixtus II, pope, martyr. Transfiguration of Christ on Mount Tabor, instituted by the Greek Church. adopted by the Latin Church.	258 700 1456
176½° MC	Sougraigne Church	(18 Aug. 19 Aug. 20 Aug.	St Helena, Empress, mother of Constantine.) 'The Apparition of the Cross' to the Emperor Constantine. Samuel, prophet. St Amator, servant of the BVM. St Louis, bishop of Toulouse.	328 312 1295
180° 4th ✭ MC C	Source de la Madeleine. Fontaine des Amours	23 Aug.	Ceres, goddess. SS Claudius, Asterius, Neon, three brothers and two women, Domnina and Theonilla, martyred in Cilicia.	 285
186° +	Hill (439m) above Source de la Madeleine	29 Aug.	Feast of the Decollation of St John the Baptist.	
192½° 1st ✭	La Soulane Hill	(4 Sep. 5 Sep. 6 Sep.	Moses, prophet) St Onesiphorus, martyr, friend of St Paul. Zechariah, prophet.	
213½° 3rd ✭	Mount Cornes peak. River Blanque joins the River Sals	(25 Sep. 26 Sep. 27 Sep. (28 Sep.	St Cleophas, disciple of Our Lord at Emmaus, possibly husband of Mary Cleophas. St Firminus, bishop, martyr, disciple of St Saturnin of Toulouse.) SS Cyprian and Justina, martyrs. SS Cosmos and Damian, Anthimus, Leontius, Euprepious, brothers and martyrs. Baruch, prophet. St Exuperius bishop of Toulouse.	 c.290 c.297 416)
229° 2nd ✭	Hill above RLB near la Fajole (480m) overlooking Bordeneuve	12 Oct.	St Cyprian and Felix, bishops, martyrs. St Wilfrid, patron of bakers, archbishop, patron of York.	c.482 709
236° 2nd ✭	Source ■ below Pic de Pidobre	19 Oct. (20 Oct. (21 Oct.	– St Mary Salome, sister of the BVM. (20th according to the Rev Owen, usually the 22nd.) St Ursula, and virgin martyrs.	 453)
247° 4th ✭ MC	Montferrand Château	30 Oct.	Mars, god. Dedication of King Solomon's Temple. St Marcellus, centurion, martyr.	298

Degree	Location	Date	Event	AD
254°	Tomb and ruin of Pontils	6 Nov.	St Protasius 1st bishop of Lausanne. St Melanius, bishop of Rennes. St Leonard, confessor, patron of prisoners.	500 530 559
256° 4th ✩	Ancient mine on slopes of the Col de Bazel	8 Nov.	'Four Crowned Martyrs' at Rome.	304
260¹/₂° MC	Pech Cardou peak and RLB Church	12 Nov.	St Rufus, 1st bishop of Avignon. St Nilus.	 c.450
261¹/₂° MC	Col de Bazel peak	13 Nov. 14 Nov.	St Mitrius (Merre), patron of Aix in Provence, guardian of the vines. — —	 304
270° 1st ✩ MC C	Fauteuil du Diable. Source of the Circle	22 Nov.	Diana, goddess of hunting. St Caecilia, virgin, martyr, patron of music.	 230
279¹/₂° +	Source du Pontet	1 Dec. 2 Dec.	Nahum, prophet. St Eligius (Eloi), bishop, patron of goldsmiths and metalworkers, also of horses. Held high post at the Court of Dagobert I. —	 665
280¹/₂° +	Roque Nègre	3 Dec.	Rhea, earth goddess. Zephaniah prophet. St Lucius (LLes ab Coel of Welsh triads.) British Christian king.	 182
282° 3rd ✩		4 Dec.	Minerva, goddess. St Barbara, virgin, martyr, patron of fortifications.	 306
283° 3rd ✩	Château Blanchefort	5 Dec.	St Bassus, bishop, martyr at Nice.	3rd C
284° 3rd ✩	Favies ruin	6 Dec.	St Nicholas, bishop, patron of children.	342
305° 2nd ✩	Le Falga ruins	26 Dec.	St Stephen, protomartyr.	34
309° 2nd ✩	Peyre Picade Source	30 Dec. 30 Dec. (31 Dec.	St Liberius I, bishop of Ravenna. S.S. Sabinus, bishop of Assisi, martyr and Others. Vesta, goddess of the hearth. St Silvester, pope, in his pontificate the Roman Empire became Christian by the conversion of Constantine.)	c.206 c.303 335
316¹/₂° HD	Jaffus ruins (between Jaffus and L'Aram ruin)	6 Jan. 7 Jan.	Epiphany. The bringing of the child Jesus back out of Egypt. St Lucian, priest, martyr.	 206
321° 4th ✩ HD	L' Aram ruin	11 Jan. (12 Jan.	St Hyginus, pope. St Theodosius, abbot. St Arcadius, martyr.)	144 529 260

Degree	Location	Date	Event	AD
330¹/₂° Y	Roc d'en Clots and ruins at Borde du Loup	20 Jan. 21 Jan.	Juno, goddess. St Fabian, Pope, martyr. St Sebastian, martyr. St Agnes, martyr.	236 287 305
340° 1st ✮ MC	Rennes le Château Church	30 Jan.	St Bathilde, queen of Clovis II.	669
341¹/₂° 1st ✮ ■	La Maurine Source	31 Jan. 1 Feb. (2 Feb.	St Melangell, patroness of hares. Februa, goddess. St Severus bishop of Ravenna. St Bridget. Oimelc. Candlemas.)	389 540
349° MC	Capia ruins	8 Feb.	St Juventius, bishop of Pavia.	2ndC
355¹/₂° 3rd ✮ MC	Jendous Source ■	14 Feb. 15 Feb.	St Valentine, priest, martyr. Pan, god. Lupercalia sacrifice of goats and dogs.	270

—   Denotes that I do not know a relevant saint.

( )   The day of eve or morrow, which I have sometimes used in the following text when it seems to be more appropriate.

+   Cross of Cardinal Points.

C   Cross in the Valley.

HD   Halves of the Druidic Year recorded around the Cross.

MC   Maltese Cross.

Y   A Druidic Year Marker.

✮   Pentagram.

■   Source Captée.

The Cross of the Cardinal Points

This is marked by the following:

West

8¹/2° La Pique. 28 February 'The Finding of the Child Jesus in the Temple.'

As our Cross is between 8° and 8$\frac{1}{2}$° East of true North this prominent little peak is within $\frac{1}{2}$° of being exactly due West of the centre of our Cross, it overlooks the land where in the past there was much pasturage and less forestation, and would have been a good vantage point to look for somebody in the valleys below. Thus the dedication here is very apt.

Many people have been puzzled by the map in the Rev Boudet's book in which he wrongly called the stream in the lower part of the valley of the Homme Mort the 'Trinque Bouteille'. This was rightly thought to be a clue, and now that we have found that it has the centre of our Cross on the side of its slopes we can clink (Trinquer) bottles with Boudet.

North

279$\frac{1}{2}$° Source Du Pontet.
1st December. Prophet Nahum. St Eligius.

This is situated in the defile entrance to Rennes les Bains, and only just outside the town, it is quite likely that there was once here a smithy which would be befitting to our saint here. This alignment is within 1° and 1$\frac{1}{2}$° West of true North. The Pole Star in the Little Bear, otherwise known as the 'Little Chariot', being the star nearest to the North Pole in the heavens, is a symbol of stability for it does not appear to move, and is regarded as the Throne of Heaven with all the other stars circling around it. Though it is the brightest, it is situated at the end of the tail of the Little Bear which has traditionally seven visible stars to the naked eye, and therefore it could be taken as the seventh. Here appropriately we have the prophet Nahum (meaning compassion) the seventh in order of the twelve minor prophets. Compassion, along with Justice, are royal attributes, and the Pole Star is the symbol of the Throne of God as King of of Heaven as it was also of Jupiter, king of the gods.

St Eligius lived after our Cross was laid out, he was brought up to be a goldsmith. He made a Throne ornamented with gold and precious stones for King Clotaire II and also two fine saddles inlaid with gold for Clotaire's son King Dagobert I of whom he was a great friend. As a bishop he held a high post in this latter king's court, and it was probably because of these saddles that he became the Patron of Goldsmiths and metal workers and also horses. Owing to the great esteem in which he was held by these Merovingian kings, he was given the date nearly corresponding to the North, North Pole and throne of Heaven.

Saint Eligius who died in 516 AD was therefore given this alignment after our Cross was laid out by the Merovingians who clearly knew the tradition of our Cross. In that excellent booklet *Les deux Rennes, le mystère Boudet* by D F Moula and F Sese the authors point out that the Grotto of the Garden which Abbot Saunière made outside his church strongly resembles that which shelters the ancient Source du Pont (or Pontet) at Campagne-les-Bains nearby. They wonder whether Saunière had placed a copy of the latter in his own garden. A very good observation, as actually this shows that he was giving us a clue to the Campange (Country) at (Rennes) les Bains, where there is also a source Du Pontet. This is situated near to the true North of our cross, and roughly indicates its vertical axis, and there is another source at Campagne les Bains which suggests the source of the Madeleine and its horizontal axis.

280½° Roque Nègre.
3rd December. St Lucius, 182 AD

We will mention here the above marker which is a ½° to the West of the Source du Pontet. It is interesting that Lucius, a British Prince, obtained missioners from Pope Eleutherus the IXth bishop of Rome. St Lucius is claimed to have later gone to Cloire in Switzerland to preach the Gospel and he is their patron saint.

East

186° Hill (439m) above the Source of the Madeleine.
29th August, Feast of the Decollation of St John the Baptist.

The Source of the Madeleine beside the River Blanque marks the eastern arm of our cross, and this alignment passes through the same river where probably many early Christians were baptised, and perhaps others by the local Druids before them.

South

99° La Ferrière Source Captée.
30th May

The traditional date of the death of King Arthur killed while fighting the Saxons. He bore a cross and an image of the Virgin Mary on his shield. This alignment is within ½° to 1° of true South. In the same manner as the hero of the early Christian Church the Emperor Constantine has been placed at the top alignment of our Cross, due South we have the renowned British hero King Arthur, who though not one of the leading nobles, was chosen because of his talents as a war leader to lead them in their battles against the invading heathen Saxons. Nennius, in his *Historia Britonum c.*800 AD states that Arthur lived at the beginning of the 6th century, and according to one report is supposed to have died in 542 AD. It is more than coincidence that in later times this date was chosen for the burning of St Joan of Arc at the stake.

IV Pentagrams

First Pentagram of Religions and the Moon Goddess Diana

With the cross of the four cardinal directions is usually associated the pentagram of the five elements, because the figure four is followed by five. Together this symbolises the Creation in Space, or the Microcosmic man, bound to the cross of form. When two of the angles of the pentagram are uppermost it represents the head of an animal with two horns, which is a creature of Nature.

With one angle only at the top, we have the Microcosmic man. His head is placed in the uppermost angle, and his arms and legs are outstretched in a saltire cross in the others. The figure is shown in a circle representing the heavens, and portrays the Son of God, the Hero, who has mastered his animal instincts by his courage and will power. This is Homo Sapiens, man with a developed individuality who has freed himself, and he lives by spirit rather than by nature. If we are to find a pentagram of the microcosm in our cross we would expect to find its top angle pointing northwards. for there is situated the Pole Star, the only celestial body that is apparently stationary, whilst all the others move around it. Therefore it stood for the throne of the unchanging, everlasting, supreme God, or His regent upon earth like the emperor of China. We have already seen how St John alluded to the 24 Elders around the throne of God in his book of Revelations. Even though we now know that it is the earth that turns, nevertheless the Pole Star still represents the line of its axis, which is practically static. This 'permanence' was thus taken by ancient peoples to represent the supreme God and his all-seeing eye, whilst the rotating stars are the cycle of Nature, the Wheel of Transformation. The shepherds of Chaldea called the stars the celestial 'sheep', but they observed that some of them on the path of the zodiac, occasionally turned back and went against the general flow of the 'sheep', these they named after the 'goats', which are more independent than sheep. The celestial 'goats' or planets, because of their occasional retrogression were supposed to have 'individuality', therefore from their movements omens were derived, out of which developed the art of astrology.

We will return to the pentagram of the Microcosmic man in which his feet in the lower two angles now point roughly to the south-east and south-west, because his head is in the north.

It is in the spring and summer that nature thrives in our climate, whilst in autumn and winter the vegetation dies down, food becomes difficult to find, and the nights become longer and the days colder. For mankind this is the time of reduced physical activity and longer confinement to their homes.

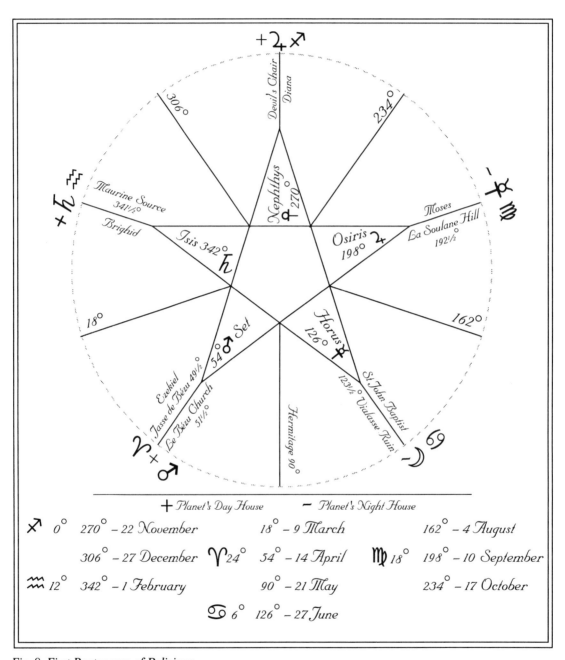

Fig. 8. First Pentagram of Religions
and the moon goddess Diana.

50

So the ancient people of very early times, being restricted for long periods in their huts, especially in the far north, reflected upon their existence and environment, from which arose the beginning of our Cosmic mythology.

Placing the Pentagram

We will now put the top angle of the pentagram to the northern arm of our Cross which is marked by the Devil's Chair. Ideally we would now expect to find the other angles at intervals of 72° apart; thus as our northern arm of the Cross is at 270° in the Calendar, the other angles of the pentagram should be at, 54°, 126°, 198° and 342° respectively.

We will start with 342°, which angle corresponds to the right hand of the Microcosmic man, and work around in a deasul manner (the reason for which will later become apparent) and find the closest alignments to these.

342° – 1/2° = 341 1/2° La Maurine Source Captée.
In Aquarius   *1st February St Severus, bishop of Ravenna 389 AD.*
                  St Bridget patroness of milking 540 AD.
                  (2nd February. Oimelc. Candlemas.)

-2° (340° Rennes Le Château Church
                  30th January. St Bathilde, Queen of Clovis II. 669 AD)

St Bridget was the christianised form of the Celtic goddess Brighid (the exalted one), and was the same as Suleva the mother goddess of the Gauls. This goddess had 19 priestesses who maintained the sacred fire which burnt perpetually, unlike all the other fires that had to be annually extinguished and re-lit, from that which was rekindled by the Druids.

This everlasting fire was surrounded by a hedge within which no man was allowed to enter. Hence her epithet in Gaul, Belisama (most brilliant).

Were these priestesses representative of the Metonic Cycle? In which case one would expect this fire to have been rekindled at the beginning of each 19 year period.

The morrow is the time of 'The Purification of the Virgin Mary', because in Pagan times it was the earth that was purified after winter for the growth of the crops. The sacred fire is the symbol of purification which gave rise to the carrying of candles at Candlemas.

St Bathilde was born in England, and as a child taken prisoner in a war, afterwards she was sold as a slave in France, then King Clovis II, son of Dagobert I married her and made her his Queen. Though she lived after our Cross was originally laid out, I include her memorial as this alignment is very important, taken with the other late attribution to St Eligius whose marker aligns to within 1 1/2° of true North, it proves that the Merovingians knew all about our Cross. Also this alignment to the church at Rennes le Château proves that they considered the latter site to be of great importance, it seems to confirm the traditional view that Rennes le Château was the original site of Rhedae, and not another site in the land below, as has been suggested. Clearly this saint's day is an artificial one to suit the alignment, rather than the actual day of her death, as must also have been the case of St Eligius' feast day.

270° Devil's Chair.

In Sagittarius   22nd November, Diana.
St Caecilia Patron of Music, virgin, martyr 230 AD

Diana was a virgin and the Roman goddess of hunting, this being the time of the chase of wild boar etc. As the mother goddess she was Diana of the Ephesians, who has been compared to the Irish De Ana (mother of the gods), this Diana wore a turreted crown, and was considered to be the 'goddess of fortifications'.

This is appropriate to this alignment of the northern arm of our Cross, which if continued from the Devil's Chair falls on the Château of Serres erected on the site of the old Visigothic fort. Serres is situated outside the entrance to our Valley, whilst the Château Blanchefort and Château Montferrand guarded it on either side.

198° -5$\frac{1}{2}$° = 192$\frac{1}{2}$° La Soulane Peak.

In Virgo   5th September St Onesiphorus.
6th September Prophet Zechariah.
(4th September Memorial of Moses.)

Here I prefer to take the eve, which would also fall on this mount. Moses the lawgiver and founder of the nation of Israel was lifted as a baby out of the Nile (here our river Sals) to later as a man and leader of his people, receive the Tablets of the Law on Mount Siniai (here La Soulane).

126° -2$\frac{1}{2}$° = 123$\frac{1}{2}$° La Vialasse ruin.

In Cancer   24 June. Midsummer's day. St John the Baptist.
25 June. St Prosper of Aquitaine. 466 AD.

The marker is an ancient ruin on the hillside due East of La Vialasse village, which is situated on the River Blanque, and up to this ruin goes a track.

Here we have St John the Baptist who is so popular in this region.
St Prosper was a renowned scholar who wrote against the Pelagian heresy, he was a Father of the Church, and a keen defender of the doctrines of Grace and here the descent of Grace and the Holy Spirit is appropriate as we shall see.

54° -2$\frac{1}{2}$° = 51$\frac{1}{2}$° Le Bézu Church.

In Aries   11th April St Antipas 'the faithful witness', bishop   180 AD
11th April St Leo the great, pope   461 AD
12th April St Sabas the Goth, martyr   372 AD

St Leo persuaded Attila, King of the Huns not to attack Rome.

-4$\frac{1}{2}$° 49$\frac{1}{2}$° La Jasse de Bézu.

9th April. St Mary Cleophas.
10th April. Prophet Ezekiel.

This falls between the day of St Mary wife of Cleophas who came with the Virgin Mary and others to Gaul in the Foundation story of the Celtic Church and that of the prophet Ezekiel.

His was the vision of the New Temple of the Kingdom of the Heavens and the celestial Cherubim in their fiery wheels of the constellations of the royal stars Aquarius, Taurus, Leo and Scorpio (for which Aquila is substituted).

The Jasse de Bézu as we shall see later was a very important and early landmark. The church of Bézu which was placed here to christianise it is more apt.

We have now found the pentagram with the following anniversaries on its points:

	Location	House
Brighid — Who represents the old Celtic religion	Maurine Spring	Aquarius. Saturn
Diana — Who represents the Roman religion	Devil's Chair	Sagittarius. Jupiter
Moses — Who represents the Jewish religion	Soulane Peak	Virgo. Mercury
St John the Baptist — The forerunner, as the commencement of Christianity	Vialasse ruin	Cancer. Moon
Ezekiel — The descent of the Kingdom of Heaven on Earth, as Jesus taught, or the temple of the New Jerusalem of which Ezekiel prophesied, and the reign of the Messiah.	La Jasse de Bézu	Aries. Mars

In this then we have got a real magical pentagram which I will call the pentagram of Religions and the Moon goddess Diana for she is at its apex and at the point of St John is the mansion of the Moon the sign of Cancer. (See Fig. 8.)

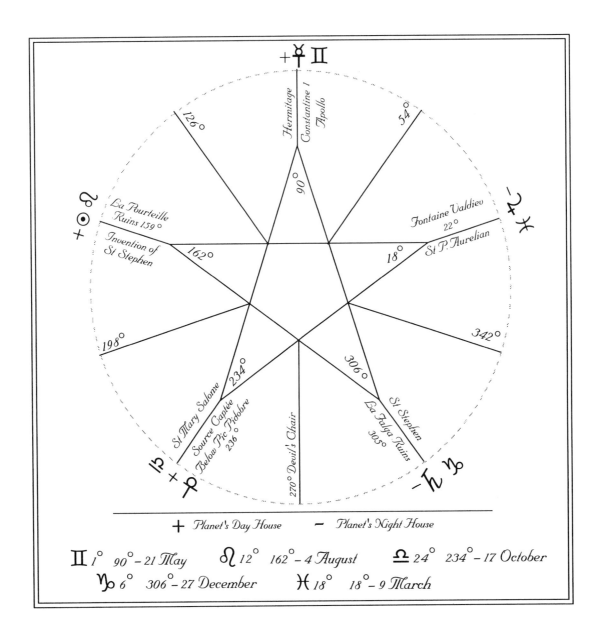

Fig. 9. Second Pentagram of the Church
    and the sun god Apollo.

54

Second Pentagram of the Church and the sun god Apollo

We have already found our first pentagram with its apex on the northern arm of our cross, which is the bottom since it is oriented towards the South, hence Saunière's clue of the inverted cross on the Visigothic Pillar under the statue of Our Lady of Lourdes. If we now place the top of another pentagram on the upper arm of the cross we have:

90° l' Ermitage, (The Hermitage).
In Gemini   21st May, Emperor Constantine I.
*   St Hospitius. Apollo.*

On this day the sun enters the sign of Gemini whose ruler is Mercury, but this sign was associated with Apollo the god of the sun by the Romans. The Emperor Constantine the Great founded the Christian Church as the official religion of the Roman Empire, Saunière has emphasised this with his translation in French of the In Hoc Signo motto of Constantine on the Holy Water Stoup below the four angels making the sign of the Cross, and above the Devil, all suggesting the cross in our valley.

It is related in an anonymous panegyric delivered shortly after the event that in 310 AD Constantine visited a famous temple of Apollo which was situated near the road from Langres to Tréves, were he had a vision of this god who offered his protection and victory in the forthcoming battles and said that he would crown him with laurel leaves. He thus became a devotee of the sun god.

Two years later he was to have the famous vision of the cross above the midday sun which spurred him and his men on to the victory at Rome, after which he became a Christian, which may explain why this day has been selected for his memorial.

At Nice from whence St Celsus came (actually from Cimiez nearby) we have the festival of the famous hermit St Hospitius who died in 580 AD. His name is immortalized in that of the peninsular of St Ospizio between Nice and Monaco. He was alive at the time that our cross was laid out, but was it a deliberate or fortuitous coincidence that his memorial day is that which aligns with our Hermitage?

18° + 4° = 22° Fontaine Valdieu and les Boudous ruins
*   13th March. St Eupraxia, virgin, 410 AD.*
*   (12th March. St Paul Aurelian, bishop, died around his centenary*
*   in 573 AD.)*
*   St Gregory the Great, pope, 540 - 604 AD.*

The saint on the eve of our marker is St Paul Aurelian, bishop of that area in Brittany where afterwards rose the city of St Pol-de-Leon, who was the son of a noble Briton of Wales. He sailed to Armorica with 12 priests, where owing to his missionary activities many idol temples were destroyed, and afterwards he was appointed bishop by the Frank Emperor Childebert.

St Gregory became famous as founder of a school of plain chant, and for sending St Augustine to England to combat Pelagianism, and to convert the Saxons and gain their submission to the Pope. Both these saints lived after the formation of our Cross, so these alignments giving us the pentagrams may well have been added later by the Merovingians.

306 -1° = 305° Le Falga ruins.
In Capricorn   *(Eve. 25th December. Birth of sun god Apollo and Jesus.)*
                           26th December. St Stephen, protomartyr.

Here we have the memorial of the first Christian martyr. I will mention here another alignment, though rather far from our marker on this point.

306° + 3° = 309°. Peyre Picade Source.
                           30th December. St Liberius I, bishop of Ravenna. c.206 AD.
                           S.S. Sabinus, bishop of Assisi, martyr and Others, c.303 AD.
                           (31st December. Vesta, goddess of the hearth.
                           St Silvester, pope, 335 AD.)

Vesta as goddess of the hearth and every sacrificial fire was worshipped with Janus at every religious service. He as the god of the door opened it and she closed it. Though this is not the day of her festival (9th of July), because that of Janus the opener of the year is on the 1st of January, Mr Crow has appropriately placed her here in his booklet *The Calendar.*

Our marker for this point of the pentagram corresponds to the 26th of December and the memorial of St Stephen the protomartyr, following Christmas and the birth of the Sun god. Just as this is the last day of the old year so it represents the end of paganism and the dawn of Christianity in the Roman empire. This was brought about by the self-sacrifice of the early Christian martyrs who refused to worship idols, and established themselves in the pontificate of St Silvester with the conversion of the Emperor Constantine.

234° + 2° = 236° Source Captée below the Pic de Pidobre.
In Libra   *19th October. — I find no relevant saint here.*
                           (237° 20th October Mary Salome sister of the Virgin Mary.
                           According to the source of the Rev Owen, generally on the 22nd.)
                           (238° 21st October. St Hilarion, abbot 371 AD.)
                           St Ursula and 11,000 virgin martyrs 453 AD.

We have here one of the Marys so beloved by the Celtic Church, who figures in the Provençal legend which was the founding story of their tradition. The following day is that of St Hilarion, abbot, and disciple of St Anthony Hermit in the North African desert, with whom our Cross is so strongly associated, also St Ursula and her virgin martyrs about whom we will have more to say later. 234° the alignment from this point falls exactly on the church of St Anne at Arques which we will discuss later.

   Though it is a little wide of this point of the Pentagram I will include here the little hill immediately above the Bordeneuve and Rennes les Bains as it is interesting.

234° -5° = 229° Hill above Rennes les Bains. (480m) near La Fajole Berg, overlooking Bordeneuve.
                           12th October. SS Cyprian and Felix, bishops, martyrs, c.482 AD.
                           St Wilfrid, patron of bakers, archbishop, patron of York, 709 AD.

Saints Cyprian and Felix suffered for their Christian belief under the Vandals in Africa. St Wilfrid lived after our cross was arranged and died in 709 AD, he helped Dagobert when he was in exile either in Ireland or Scotland, took him to England and cared for him, then brought Dagobert back to Austrasia, the eastern kingdom of the Merovingians to become their king.

162° -3 = 159° La Pourteille ruins.
In Leo   *1st August. Lugnasad. St Peter in chains.*
                               (160° 2nd August. St Stephen, pope and martyr. 257 AD.)
                               (161° 3rd August. Invention of St Stephen 415 AD.)

We have here Lugnasad, and St Peter in chains which we will find corresponds with the dedication of the church at Serres when the calendar is placed in a clockwise manner around our Cross.

I think that we can also include the 3rd of August, the morrow of our alignment as 160° the day of the Pope Stephen. This is the day of the Invention of the bodies of St Stephen, the protomartyr and Nicodemus, Gamaliel, and his son Abibas, to whom the church at Sougraigne is dedicated.

The dedication of this church seems to be intended as a reminder of the cross hidden in our valley, and Stephen is the Greek for a crown. The golden crowns of kings clearly symbolise the sun at its greatest strength in summer, and likewise the first martyr St Stephen and the later pope and martyr of the same name, are summits of the Christian Church. The leonine characteristic of strength and ferocity gives its name to the house of the sun in Leo, whose main star is Regulus Latin for a minor king or prince.

By the time of the invention of St Stephen, about a hundred years after the Emperor Constantine had recognised Christianity, the Church was well established throughout the Roman Empire.

162° +2° = 164° Source near Les Carbounières
                  6th August. Transfiguration of Christ, instituted by the Greek Church
                  in 700 AD and by the Latin in 1456, and therefore too late for our cross.

Thus we have, in tracing, our second pentagram in a clockwise manner:

1   The Emperor Constantine the Great, establisher of the Church, representing
       Kings.

2   The British missionary and bishop Paul Aurelian, and the bishop of Rome,
       Pope Gregory the Great, representing **Bishops**.

3   The first Christian martyr, St Stephen, representing **Martyrs**.

4   (A) Mary Salome who according to the legend of Veroli in Italy, of which she is
           the patroness, died in a cave nearby, as a solitary. She is however claimed
           by the Provençal legend.
       (B) St Hilarion, abbot and disciple of St Anthony Hermit is probably more
           correct here, of such universal popularity, representing Monastics and
           Hermits.

5   Invention of the bodies of St Stephen, Nicodemus, Gamaliel, and Abibas. This
       is therefore the place of the communion of Saints, and in order to contact
       them, pilgrimages were made to their tombs, or churches holding their remains,
       representing here **Relics**.

To distinguish this second pentagram from the first, and because it so clearly portrays Christian images, I have called it the Pentagram of the Church, and sun god Apollo because he is at its Apex with Leo the house of the Sun.

Our first pentagram shows some of the older religions, forerunners of Christianity, in which the Spirit of Christ was present before the Messiah Jesus brought them to their fulfilment.

There we saw that we could include the point of St John the Baptist's birthday in Cancer, and also the summer solstice which occurs three days before. Diana the moon goddess is at the apex of the pentagram in a day house, and Cancer is the night house of the Moon.

At the point of Brighid and St Bridget on the morrow is the festival of light, Candlemas, that of the purification of the earth, which falls in Aquarius whose ruler Saturn is intimately associated with agriculture and the earth.

This first pentagram is then especially connected with the Moon. Similarly in the second pentagram on the point of the foot which corresponds to that of St John the Baptist in the first, we have on the eve of our marker Christmas, the birth of Jesus and also of the Sun. Also on the point where we had Candlemas, we have the Invention of St Stephen, and just prior to that Lugnasad in Leo, mansion of the Sun.

So this second pentagram rightly belongs to the Sun. It is fitting that the moon goddess Diana, the Greek Artemis is at the apex of the first pentagram, and that Apollo the Sun god and twin of Artemis is at the apex of the second

We see that in each pentagram there are two night houses and three day houses of the planets and major luminaries, which is in accord with the Pythagorean idea that the number *two* was the first feminine, and number *three* the first masculine one.

The three natural positions of the sun, at rise, noon and set, I think are the origin of our Pythagorean Triangle of Spirit, visualised as being formed from them. These were the first indicators of the time for prehistoric man, which divided the day-time into two parts, thus sunrise, noon and sunset were the times of worship for the solar peoples.

Later they became accustomed to judging the sun's position in the sky, the midpoint of each of these, thus dividing the day into four parts which the Romans knew as:

- Mane — Sunrise to between 9 and 10 a.m. our time.
- Ad Meridiem — Forenoon
- De Meridie — Afternoon until 3 or 4 p.m.
- Suprema — From then until sun-set.

These five points of observation of the sun at sunrise, noon and sunset, with the two intermediary observations are roughly preserved in the five middle times of the seven periods of Christian prayer; at Prime, Terce, Sext, None, and Vespers. (See Fig. 13.)

In this second pentagram the lower angles or feet ideally should be at 234° and 306° instead of the 236° and 305° of our markers. These former positions fall on the 17th of October and the 27th of December respectively, and this is a remarkable proof of intent for anyone who may be doubting our alignments as purely coincidental, for of the four Evangelists, we have the feast of St Luke falling on the morrow of the 17th of October, the 18th, and that of St John on the 27th of December. It is very befitting to see the feet of this pentagram of the Christian Church supported by these two Evangelists of love and healing.

58

We have found two pentagrams in our calendar around our cross oriented to the North and South on its vertical or Meridianal axis; that of the extremes of elevation at the solstices, marking the beginning of the hottest and coldest seasons of the year. The ancients however paid great respect to the four Cardinal points of the Four Winds which of course include the East and West as well as the North and South. This East to West line represents the horizontal axis of our cross, that of the two equinoxes when the length of the day is equal to that of the night, and when the ecliptic crosses the celestial equator.

We would therefore expect to find two more pentagrams, one with its apex to the east of sunrise, and another to the West of sunset, at the time of the two equinoxes.

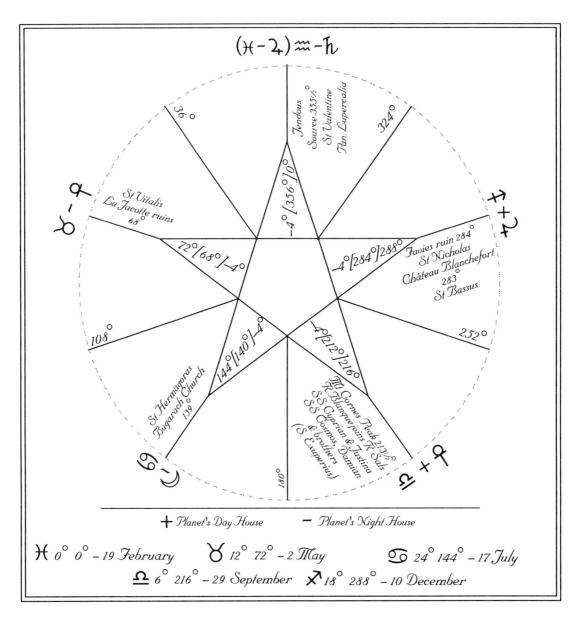

Fig. 10. Third Pentagram of Fertility and the god Pan.

Third Pentagram of Pan and Fertility.

We have not got an exact marker for our cross in the West, which falls vaguely on the Homme Mort. The nearest marker is the Jendous Source at 355½° instead of 360°, this however makes a very good pentagram with its other markers. They are as follows:

360° – 41/2° = 3551/2° Jendous Source Captée.
In Aquarius   14th February. St Valentine, priest and martyr 270 AD
*   15th February Pan. Lupercalia. Juno.*

We have here the ancient custom of young people declaring their love to each other, it otherwise has no apparent connection with St Valentine. It is thought that it is a custom similar to, if not actually arising from the Lupercalia, one of the most important of the festivals in Rome.

   This month of February (Latin *Februarius* from *Februo* 'to purify') was dedicated to Juno also called Februata because of the purification of the earth at this time, and also to the rural god Pan, which were the gods to whom the Lupercalia was sacred. At this festival, goats and dogs were sacrificed, originally as an offering of the shepherds, like the paschal lamb of the Palestinian shepherds. Note that Saunière has placed on this arm of the cross the shepherdess and patron of the young agricultural workers St Germaine, which is most appropriate.

   This apex of the third pentagram dedicated to the shepherd god Pan and Juno is clearly connected with the fertility both of animals and the land.

72° - 4° = 68° La Jacotte ruins
In Taurus   28th April. St Vitalis, martyr, patron of Ravenna.

This saint brings to mind the Empress Galla Placidia who seems to have connected her town of Ravenna with Rennes les Bains and the Holy Valley. This name Vitalis clearly suggests the Latin *vita* meaning 'life'.

144° - 5° = 139° Bugarach Church
In Cancer   12th July. St Hermagoras disciple of St Mark, the first bishop of
*   Aquileia.*

The name Hermagoras combines that of Hermes and Agora. Hermes was the god of trade, being that of roads, and the travellers, most of whom were merchants who naturally were to be found at the place of assembly or the market place which is the meaning of the Greek word *Agora*. Among the Celts as we know from Ireland, fairs were generally held at the ancient mounds and circles, burial places of the indigenous people which frequently dated back to Megalithic times. On these festive occasions games, marriages, feasting, trading, and even the legal assizes took place and the traditions and laws were explained. Therefore at this point we have Hermes and Agora suggesting fairs and trade.

61

216° - 2¹/2° = 213¹/2° Mount Cornes peak. Junction of the Rivers Blanque and Sals.

In Libra   *26th September. SS Cyprian and Justina, martyrs.*
                                    27th September. SS Cosmos, Damian, Anthimus, Leontius, and
                                    Euprepius, brothers and martyrs, c. 297 AD.
                                    (28th September. Baruch, prophet. St Exuperius bishop
                                    of Toulouse. 416 AD).
                                    (29th September. St Michael and of all Angels).

This is the memorial to the two martyrs Cyprian and Justina under the purge of the Emperor Diocletian. The Rev S Baring Gould considers the story of their lives in *The Acts* to have been a Christian romance built around their memory, however, St Naziarizen recognised in Cyprian the great St Cyprian of Carthage, the philosopher who was converted to Christianity in his old age.

The story tells how St Cyprian was a famous magician at Antioch in Syria. As an infant he was consecrated to Apollo and at the age of ten made an Athenian citzen, was the torch bearer of Demeter, and wore the white mourning for the Maiden (Persephone). He went on to travel to Phrygia to learn astronomy and astrology. In other words, he became a perfect adept in the magical arts, and the story relates how he was consulted by a youth called Aglaïdes who requested him to help win the favours against her will of a Christian maiden called Justina. Despite all the evil magic that Cyprian could perform, and the devils that he sent to persuade Justina, he was powerless against this pure Christian girl, which made such an impression on Cyprian that he was converted to Christianity.

As this marker lies between the 26th and 27th of September we have in nearly all Latin Martyrologies on the 27th the five brother martyrs SS Cosmos, Damian, Anthimius, Leontius and Euprepius, but in the Orthodox Church they are celebrated on July 1st.

SS Cosmos and Damian were physicians who according to the legend took no fees, and became the patrons of surgeons and barbers, and were decapitated at Ægis in Cilicia around 297 AD because being Christians they refused to worship the idols of the gods.

What is interesting is that we have five (or a pentagram of) saints, and brothers which suggests the five intercalary days of a Coptic style year. As the Autumn equinox falls on the 23rd of September, if this was taken to be the first of the intercalary days then this fifth would fall on the 27th of September where we now have the memorial of these brothers to whom would originally have been allocated a day for each saint, and the year would have begun on our 28th of September. We will discover later how this alignment is used to mark the angle of the axis of Rogations and that of Christ's Ascension.

Though the Mount Cornes marker is more appropriate to a pentagram with its apex at 360°, the rest are more in accord with ours which has the Jendous source 355¹/2°.

(25th September. St Cleophas, disciple of Jesus.
St Firminus, bishop, martyr, disciple of St Saturnin of Toulouse.)

The junction of two rivers was always considered a very holy place amongst the ancients, as for example in India where the Jumna joins the Ganges, similarly where three roads joined was sacred to Hecate, and the cross-roads had the same significance.

In the Heavens the Ecliptic crosses the Celestial Equator at the place of the two equinoxes from which mystical image the above may be derived, thus here where the Blanque meets the Sals we have on the bank a place called the Benitier (Holy water stoup) presumably in memory of the previous acclaim given to this site.

We also have the road from Bugarach running alongside the River Blanque which here meets the road coming down from Sougraigne and follows the Sals to continue down into Rennes les Bains. On the eve there is the festival of St Cleophas, disciple of Jesus who did not recognise the resurrected Lord on the way to Emmaus, who is also thought to be the husband of St Mary Cleophas. This seems to suggest that the Christian pilgrim might receive here at the Benitier the divine blessing of the presence of Christ, even though he be unaware of it.

St Firminus a bishop and martyr being the disciple of St Saturnin of Toulouse is therefore very appropriate here.

28th September

This is the morrow of the former marker Mount Cornes where we have the prophet Baruch (Blessed) and St Exuperius of Toulouse whose name most likely comes from the latin Exubero (to abound, to produce in great abundance) which is in harmony here with the idea of sex, marriage and prosperity; a typical ancient blessing (thus Baruch).

The Mount Cornes (Latin *Cornu* 'a horn') suggests the ancient Gallic god Cernunnos who wore two antlers with torques hanging from them, and is thought to have been the Lord of Beasts. This stands for the fertility of the animals on which mankind depended for food.

29th September

Though there is no marker, this date would correspond with a site a little to the West of the peak of Mount Cornes. Here we have the day of St Michael and of all angels who cast out the devil in the form of a dragon from heaven; the Christian devil who was thought to have horns would certainly have been applied to Cernunnos and associated with Mount Cornes.

288° - 5° = 283° Château Blanchefort.
In Sagittarius   5th December. St Bassus, bishop and martyr at Nice.

The alignment with the existing ruins of the Château falls on the festival of St Bassus of Nice, appropiately the same region as that of St Celsus of the church of Rennes les Bains. The castle may have extended its enclosures from the centre of our cross and thus included the 4th of December, but in any case the adjacent fêtes are often relative. This then is the day of St Barbara, Patron saint of Fortifications, doubtless because it was also sacred to the Roman goddess of Wisdom and Patroness of Armour, Minerva.

- 4° 284° Favies ruin
*   6th December. St Nicholas, Patron of Children and Sailors, 342 AD.*

At our last point of the pentagram we therefore have St Nicholas, Patron of Children, on whose day in some countries they used to receive presents.

We can thus conclude that all the points of this third pentagram agree with its first and refer to sex and fertility which we can briefly summarize as:

1   **Courting** — St Valentine. Pan and the Lupercalia
2   **Life** — St Vitalis
3   **Marriage work and play** — St Hermagoras
4   **Fertility** — St Exuperius (Cernunnos)
5   **Children** — St Nicholas

In this pentagram we can now see why there is no marker at 360° for the western arm of our Cross, for if there were one it would fall in the sign of Pisces and we would not have for this apex the god Pan and the Lupercalia, or St Valentine's day.

The Rev Saunière seemed to know about this pentagram and gives us a clue by placing opposite St Mary Magdalen in his church the statue of St Germaine, Cousin of Pibrac, (which as we know corresponds for this arm of the cross and apex of this third pentagram). Since she was a young shepherdess and in consequence the Patron saint of young agricultural workers she seems most apt here.

Pibrac. The paternal house of St Germaine. (Postcard c. 1920.)

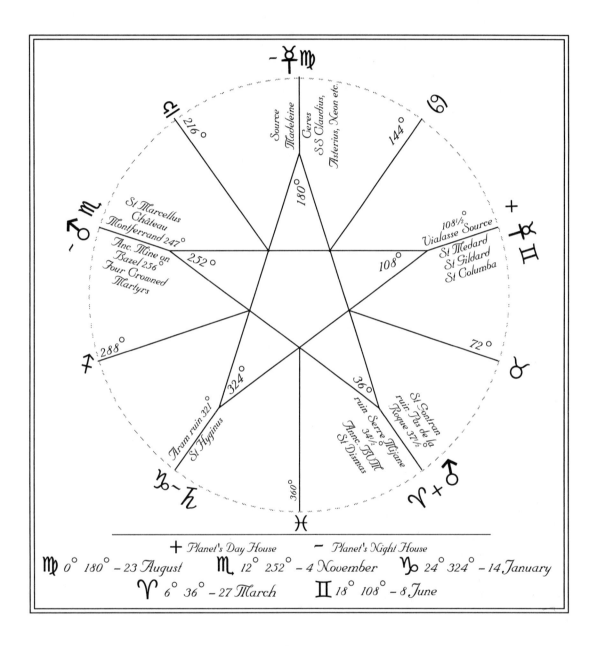

Fig. 11. Fourth Pentagram of the Virgin Mary and
  the Harvest goddess Ceres.

65

Fourth Pentagram of the Virgin Mary, Ceres and the Harvest

The apex of this pentagram will face East and therefore is marked by the Source of the Madeleine at 180° and the other points should ideally fall on 252°, 324°, 36° and 108°. We have:

180° Source of the Madeleine. Fontaine des Amours
Sun enters Virgo   *23rd August. Ceres. SS Claudius, Asterius and Neon who were*
                           three brothers and two women Domnina and Theonilla, they were
                           martyred together in Cilicia in 285 AD.

Here is Ceres goddess of the harvest, and the constellation of the Virgin holding a blade of corn which is marked by her brightest star Spica, for it is the time of the harvest. On this day, the 23rd of August, we have the memorial of SS Claudius, Asterius and Neon the three brothers who were crucified and exposed to birds of prey for their belief in Christ. Two women were marytred with them, Domnina who was stripped naked and flogged to death, whilst Theonilla was flung on the ground, tormented with thistles, lashed and drowned in the sea.

In ancient Egypt, the Alexandrian Year started (at the time of the Roman conquest in 30 BC) on the 29th of August (Julian) and therefore the first of the intercalary days fell on the 24th of August. This looks like the beginning of a year based on the ancient Alexandrian, but starting a day earlier so as to coincide with the sun entering the sign of Virgo. In this case the year would have started on the 28th of August following the five saints' days, and we see that there are three brothers and two women, just like the three brother gods and their two sisters of the ancient Egyptian intercalary days.

The dedication of this spring to St Mary Magdalen is appropriate as it is at the start of these Alexandrian intercalary days instead of in July as in the Sothic Year, and of course at the beginning of Virgo. With Ceres and Virgo at the apex of the fourth pentagram we can take it to symbolise the Harvest and Reward.

252° - 5° = 247° Château Montferrand
In Scorpio   *30th October. Mars. St Marcellus, 298 AD.*
                    Dedication of King Solomon's Temple.

This was the day of the festival of the Roman god of war, Mars, ruler of the sign of Scorpio which the sun enters on the 23rd of October. St Marcellus a centurion and Christian martyr came from an illustrious plebeian family of the Gens Claudia.

This saint is very apt here as Montferrand has always been intimately connected with Rennes les Bains which is known to have been a very popular Spa of the Romans.

The Mont ferrand or Mount Ferrand in English is clearly derived from the Latin word *Ferrum* meaning 'iron' whose planetary god is Mars, and so named because of the deposit of iron ore that was mined here. Our alignment implies that there was a Visigothic fort on the remains of which the ruined Château was built.

*An early photograph of the Source of the Circle at Rennes les Bains. (Postcard posted 1916.)
Note the fountain with its peculiar bowl above the three men on the right.*

*A later photograph of the Source of the Circle at Rennes les Bains. (Postcard c. 1920.)
This was situated below the present source.*

Rennes les Bains seen from the Circle. (Postcard c.1920.)

Jean Robin in his *Rennes le Château* (p.128) quotes from an article by Miss Myriam David a history teacher who claimed that the baths of Rennes les Bains were built by Marcellus during the Roman occupation, and the place called the 'Cross' or the 'Circle' on the large scale maps (cadastre) corresponds to the Round Temple which he constructed. If this was so then our Cross has been deliberately arranged so that St Marcellus of the alignment of Montferrand also preserves his memory. Montferrand therefore by its name, and its day in our calendar of the noble Roman Centurion St Marcellus, seems to confirm that the Valley was in Gallic times dedicated to their god of war, Camulus, which we will discuss later.

Dedication of King Solomon's Temple. 15th of Tishri. (30th October)

This festival is also on this alignment to Montferrand. In I Kings VIII we learn how Solomon dedicated his temple on the feast of the seventh month, that of Tabernacles (Lev. 23 v34). The Jewish months were lunar and therefore did not accurately correspond to those of our year. This commemoration on the 30th of October and the death of Hiram Abiff, King Solomon's architect on the 2nd have been handed down to us as the two most important ceremonies of the Operative Masons which they celebrated annually. This is very interesting here, and was doubtless known to the stonemasons who built the churches and forts of the Visigoths in this region.

252° +4° = 256° Ancient Mine on the slopes of the Col de Bazel.
8th November. The Four Crowned Martyrs at Rome. 304 AD.

There were four stonemasons amongst the 622 artisans employed in building a temple to Helios in Pannonia, who sculpted a remarkably good statue of Æsculapius, god of health, called the Saviour (Soter). They had no objection in doing this as he was analogous to Christ. This pleased the Emperor Dioclesian, however, when he learnt that they were Christians, and they refused to sacrifice to Helios, he ordered their martyrdom.

In Rome in the 4th century were discovered the bodies of four decapitated martyrs believed to be them, for whom a church was erected called 'The Quatuor Coronati'. They very soon became the Patron Saints of the Operative Guilds of Stonemasons, and they are often portrayed in Romanesque churches as crowned and having the tools of their trade at their feet. Another important alignment for the Freemasons!

Æsculapius was the Greek god of medicine, which is not inappropriate here with the healing waters of Rennes les Bains. It has been claimed that the Four Crowned Martyrs were sculptors or master metal workers of the Roman Collegia of Architects and thus the supposed forerunners of modern Freemasonry.

The former alignment as by far the most important marker, is most probably the one intended for this point of the pentagram.

324° – 3° = 321° Aram ruin
In Capricorn   *11th January. St Hyginus. pope. 144 AD*
St Theodosius 423 - 529 AD

St Hyginus' name obviously comes from Hygea (from the Greek *higeia* meaning 'health') the goddess of health personified, which is most appropriate for our valley. Likewise the name of St Theodosius means the 'gift of God'.

36° – 1¹/₂ = 341/2 Ruin on the Serre Mijane
In Aries   *25th March. Annunciation of the Blessed Virgin Mary.*
St Dismas the penitent thief who hung on the cross on the right
side of Jesus.
Memorial of Melchizedek.

+1¹/₂° = 37¹/₂° Ruin at the bottom of Pas de la Roque
28 March. St Gontran, grandson of Clovis and
St Clothilde. 525 - 593 AD.

The latter ruin seems to have been a building deliberately erected by the Merovingians to record St Gontran whose memorial they may have also arranged to coincide with this point of our pentagram.

We have here the announcement of the birth of Jesus to the virtuous Virgin Mary, Dismas the repentant thief at the Crucifixion, and Melchizedek (Heb. 'King of righteousness') the most holy Priest King of Canaanite Jerusalem, who blessed Abraham.

Hebrews (VII) maintains that Jesus was not only of the tribe of Judah, but also designated by God as a high 'Priest for ever after the order of Melchizedek', and that after His supreme self-sacrifice no further sin offerings were necessary. This act of purification by the high priest on the Day of Atonement gave 'rebirth' to the priests and people. I think therefore we can associate this point with rebirth in Christ.

108° +1/2° = 1081/2° Vialasse Source Captée and Mine Ruins.
8th June. St Medard , bishop of Noyen, patron of vineyards
and St Gildard, bishop of Rouen, twins. 545 AD.
9th June. St Columba of Iona. 597 AD.

Today St Medard is more widely known in France as the Patron of Vineyards than St Merre the Guardian of the Vines. It is appropriate to find him here in the Pentagram of the Harvest and Ceres the corn goddess, representing the vintage.

Because of the late date of these saints this must have been added afterwards. Iona or Hii as it was known in ancient times was a seat of the Druids. St Columba founded there a monastery around 565 AD, and it remained the stronghold of the Culdees until taken over by the Benedictines in the 13th century. St Columba's name came from the Latin *Columba* meaning a 'dove' or 'pigeon', and was clearly chosen because it is the emblem of the Holy Spirit which descended on Jesus at his baptism by John. We can associate this point with gifts of the Holy Spirit. The Roman philosopher Boethus (475 - 524 AD) who was an official at the court of Theodoric King of the Ostrogoths informs us that when Alaric the Goth sacked Rome in 410 AD he presented certain manuscripts to the library at Iona. (This was before the time of St Columba.) It is interesting to note that the Arian Christian Goths had a connection with the Celtic Church in the British Isles, thereby perhaps allowing us to accept British and Irish saints here, such as St Columba.

I think that we can summarise the points of this fourth pentagram as follows:

1   **Harvest**, the rewards of our actions and labour. Ceres. SS Claudius, Asterius etc. symbolising the end of one period (the agricultural year) and the new beginning.

2   **Struggle**, building one's moral character, dedication of the self to the Saviour. St Marcellus the noble centurion. Four Crowned Martyrs and their image of the Soter.

3   **Health**, especially spiritual. SS Hyginus and Theodosius.

4   **Rebirth**. Annunciation of the Virgin Mary. Repentance of St Dismas.

5   **Holy Spirit**, the descent of, with gifts. St Columba.

This pentagram we can attribute to the Virgin Mary, for on one of its points there is the feast of the 'Annunciation', and at the apex is Virgo, with whom she is associated.

70

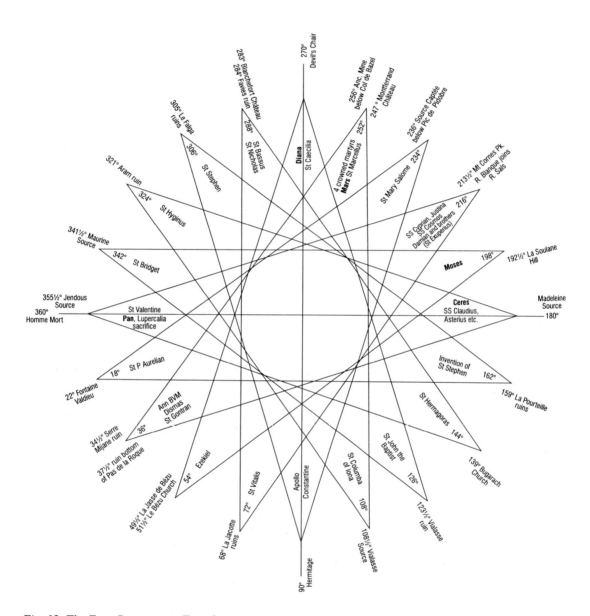

Fig. 12. The Four Pentagrams Together.

71

Fifth Pentagram of the Great Mother

We have found the Pentagrams:

First	apex at the beginning of	Sagittarius of the element	FIRE
Second	apex at the beginning of	Gemini of the element	AIR
Third	apex at the end of	Aquarius of the element	(AIR) WATER
Fourth	apex at the beginning of	Virgo of the element	EARTH

Ideally the third pentagram should begin with Pisces of the element WATER, but we found no close marker on the Homme Mort for 360°. The marker we assigned to our third pentagram was Jendous Source at $355^{1}/2°$ which is right at the end of the sign of Aquarius, only $4^{1}/2°$ from the beginning of Pisces. It appeared to be deliberate that the god Pan and goddess Juno should be at the apex of this pentagram. We can therefore take this Pentagram to belong, as it should, to Pisces and to the element Water.

There are five elements, four of which are held in the matrix of the fifth which is unaffected by them, of ETHER.

We will see how the five planets (which exclude the sun and moon) of the Five Day Week are allotted the five elements when we discuss the Ancient Egyptian pentagram. (See Fig. 8.) We would therefore expect to find a 5th pentagram corresponding to the element Ether, but this latter element being the womb of and unaffected by the other four is consequently not allotted to any of the signs of the zodiac. Where to place it? Well we have seen how the Pole Star is the only apparently stationary star in the night sky, around which all the others move, and though we oriented the first pentagram in its direction, this was to the North and not to the North Pole in the sky. We can therefore orientate the apex of the fifth pentagram to the Pole Star, which like Ether being unmoved by the other four elements, is static whilst all the other stars circle round it. Though, for comparison, we placed the planets in the figure of the first pentagram, they really belong to the fifth as their movement is independent of the apparent course of the constellations of the zodiac and other stars.

The latter the ancient Chaldeans conceived of as sheep, whilst the independent five planets which could even stop in their courses and retrograde, were typical of goats.

The apex of this fifth pentagram will obviously be assigned to Mercury and his planet, being the god of travellers, which corresponds to the element Ether.

Whilst the other four pentagrams represent the cardinal points on earth, and the four elements whose interplay make up life on our world, the fifth, being unaffected by them, can be compared to the upper and lower hemispheres of the sky. Similarly it also represents the underground of the Great Mother that holds the seeds and roots of the vegetation in the 'womb' of the earth. We can therefore allot this pentagram to the Great Mother in her two aspects as the Sky Virgin and the Earth Mother.

These four directions of the Cardinal Points and the fifth of Pole Star have always been of prime importance in the rituals of primitive magic (such as that of the northern Shamans), and those of early religions to that of the most sophisticated ones.

The Nature Spirits and the Pentagrams

We have seen how each of the first four pentagrams have a different element belonging to the zodiacal sign at the apex, (though the apex of the third pentagram falls at the end of Aquarius, it really belongs to Pisces and water). Also if one examines the other angles one finds that in each pentagram the other four points fall in zodiacal signs that happen to belong to earth, water, air and fire respectively. For example in the case of the first pentagram, with Sagittarius whose element is fire at its apex, we have (going through the pentagram anti-clockwise) Sagittarius, Fire; Aries, Fire; Virgo, Earth; Aquarius, Air; and Cancer, Water. Thus in each pentagram the predominant element at its apex, can either be pure, associating only with its like, or can mix with one or more of the others to form the Creation.

We can align to each of the first four pentagrams the names used by Paracelsus (1493 - 1541) for the pure elementals:

First pentagram	Sagittarius	FIRE	Salamanders.	
Second pentagram	Gemini	AIR	Sylphs.	
Third pentagram	Pisces*	WATER	Undines	*(instead of Aquarius)
Fourth pentagram	Virgo	EARTH	Gnomes.	

In early times, people knew the cross of the Cardinal Points, and the daily positions of the sun, and of course the North indicated by the pole star at night, so our Cross would be easily understood. But how about the pentagrams, to what would they relate? Well as we have just seen, each pentagram not only represents a different pure element, but a mixture with other elements, thus all the different types of fairies according to their habitat and activity can be allocated to one or other of these pentagrams.

These 'little folk' were fully recognised in Paganism, either as lesser gods and goddesses or as spirits of the earth, water, air and fire. It was very dangerous for instance, to plough the ground or mine the earth, as one might annoy the gnomes or the spirits of the dead, they had to be propitiated with offerings, to win their favour.

The spirits of the wells, springs and rivers were also given offerings, coins and pins were thrown into wells and springs, and strips of cloth tied to nearby bushes, for how vital is the need for fresh water. What if these sources were to dry up owing to the anger of their little spirit patrons? The spirits of the air could bring pleasant breezes or disastrous hurricanes, and they also controlled the clouds. Under this heading can also probably be counted those spirits of trees and crops that sway in the wind. They all had to be propitiated.

Lastly we have the fire spirits. It was essential to keep a fire burning in the domestic hearth, and there was the danger of uncontrolled fires, and lightning. These spirits also had to be appeased. Even though the Christian religion was adopted and the ancient gods dismissed to hell, nevertheless this belief in the power of the 'good folk' to help, or create mischief prevailed, and they were placated with offerings down to recent times. Thus these pentagrams are not just metaphysical, but on the contrary, very representative of life in general.

On his Holy Water Stoup, above the Devil holding up the water vessel and below the Angels making the sign of the cross Saunière has placed two salamanders, presumably male and female. These were found on old fonts where they stood for baptism of the Holy Spirit.

73

Salamanders were supposed to be able to withstand the heat of fire and thus became the symbol of the Fire elementals. In heraldry they signify brave and generous courage that cannot be destroyed by the fire of affliction. They were therefore in Christianity the symbols of ardent faith. François I of France adopted the salamander amidst the flames with the motto 'Nutrisco et extinguo', in the Italian original 'I nourish the good and extinguish the bad'. He placed the crowned salamander with this motto in his castle of Chambord, in the galleries of the Palace of Fontainebleau, and the Hotel St Bourg Thoroulde at Rouen. Doubtless Saunière had in mind the gift of the Countess of Chambord (from whom he received a gift), and also her late husband, as representative of the King and Queen of France.

The five lines that join the points of a pentagram to its centre form the Egyptian symbol for a star. The most important of the stars was Sothis (Sirius) which rose just before the sun when it heralded the rise of the Nile.

Sothis was considered to be a goddess, a form of Isis, which marked the beginning of the agricultural year. The ancient Solar/Lunar year was considered to have 12 months of 30 days each, making 360 days in all, which formed 72 weeks of five days each, later to be taken in pairs as the Dekans, the true tropical year has nearly $365^{1}/4$ days, thus leaving $5^{1}/4$ days unaccounted for in this year. In the ancient Egyptian myth, as related by Plutarch, we learn that the god Thoth was thought to have won these $5^{1}/4$ days in a game of draughts from the Moon god, in other words the inaccuracy of the length of the year was discovered by observation, 'draughts' symbolising the 'game' between the summer and winter halves of the year. These five days were therefore thought to be outside the calendar year, and because of their independence, contain great magical potency. Thus the five gods of the Osirian cycle, Osiris, Horus the elder, Set, Isis and Nephthys, were thought to have been born on these Epagomenal days in the above order, which were intercalated or added to the year, and every fourth year an extra day making six in all was attached. This gave us the Ancient Egyptian Wandering Year for it was still not perfect, and the months slowly travelled around the seasons. This same year was adopted by Julius Ceasar when he corrected the ancient Roman calendar, the only change to it being that its beginning was transferred from August to January.

In Fig. 8, in the first pentagram of Religions and the Moon goddess Diana, I have placed around the points the gods of the ancient Egyptian Epagomenal days in their correct order with the Goddess Isis of the alluvial land watered by Osiris as god of the Nile, at the point of St Bridget and the pagan goddess Brighid at Candlemas which was once again the time of the purification of the soil. I have also shown the planets I have allotted to these three gods and two goddesses.

By going through this pentagram in a deasul manner starting from Isis and Saturn, we have the order of the planets, and by going round it widdershins the order of the days in a five day week. (The sun's day and the moon's day being the additions to make the seven day week.) Though in the late period in which Plutarch gathered this myth, Osiris was the first to be 'born' and had his fete on the first Epagomenal day, as the chief god of this group, it is quite possible that at a very early period Isis may have come first, followed by Nephthys and so on.

In pre-dynastic times it appears that goddesses were very important, and though eventually the Patriarchy became dominant nevertheless women never completely lost their power as in other cultures. The chief example of this is that the male Pharaoh could only reign when he had alongside him his female Pharaoh of royal lineage to share his rule. The apex of the Egyptian pentagram would be that of the second day of 'Horus the Elder' the falcon god who personified the day sky and whose eyes were the sun and the moon. Appropriately he is found on the point of Cancer, house of the moon and the summer solstice in the era of Aries, when the sun is at its greatest height as it crosses the meridian at noon.

Comparison of our First Pentagram with the Egyptian		
Brighid — Mother goddess. Time of purification of the earth for crops. Purification of the BVM	**Isis** — Alluvial soil goddess annually deposited by the River Nile of her husband Osiris	**Saturn, Earth** — He was the sower of seeds in the soil
Diana — Goddess of hunting 'flying like the wind across the earth'	**Nephthys** — Edge of the valley goddess. Probably of the desert winds, sometimes cool and pleasant, otherwise hot and stifling. This would explain why she vacillated in her support of her husband Set and her brother Osiris	**Venus, Air** — The dove was sacred to Venus suggesting the element of air
Moses — meaning 'being drawn forth' from the Nile. Also the waters 'drawn aside' to let the Israelites pass out of Egypt. Similar to the Egyptian verb 'MSI', to give birth	**Osiris** — identified with the life giving waters of the Nile on which the Egyptians depended, there being very little rainfall	**Jupiter, Water** — God of thunder and lightning who caused the rains to fall
St John the Baptist — the ascetic recluse, forerunner and proclaimer of Jesus, at whose baptism the dove as the symbol of the Holy Sprit descended. Likened himself to the moon and Jesus to the sun	**Horus the Elder** — God of the highest Heaven, whose eyes were the sun and moon	**Mercury, Ether or Spirit** — messenger of the gods, guide of the dead spirits to the underworld, the unknown. His caduceus being a symbol of the sun and moon
Ezekiel — saw a vision of the Cherubim in fiery wheels. Prophet who ranted at the people and tried to inspire them with his high ideals	**Set** — The force of opposition, (like the Hindu Shiva the 'destroyer') which brings about the struggle of life and change. Was later thought of as the Devil. Set was the desert god of oppressive heat and sterility	**Mars, Fire** — God of war and struggle. The upward striving of vegetation. The one who by his energy starts events and growth, March, the first Roman month

In the above order of the elements which here appear to be appropriate for the five Egyptian gods we have Earth, Water, Fire, Air and Ether or Spirit. This is the Indian order and not that later used in Europe in which Air precedes Fire. This seems to have been noticed by Plutarch when he tells us about their birthdays, for he says "Upon the third (day) Typho (i.e. Set) came into the world, being born neither at the proper time, nor by the right place, but forcing his way through a wound he had made in his mother's side". (*De Iside et Osiride* XII). Plutarch probably thought that Set should have been born on the fifth day and his wife Nephthys on the third, which would then have given the order of the elements as he knew them when read through the pentagram from Isis as the Earth. In agreement with this order and the Egyptian gods the others have been placed.

76

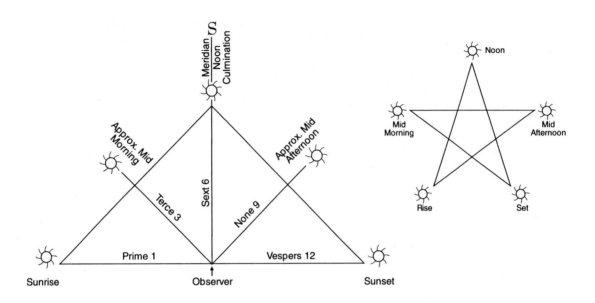

Fig. 13. Solar Divisions and Daily Prayers.

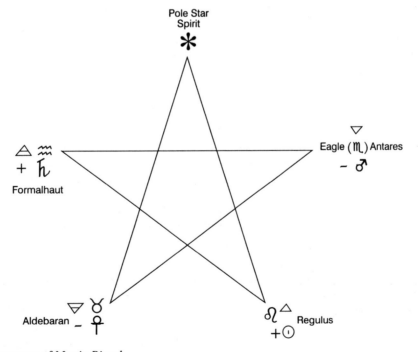

Fig. 14. Pentagram of Magic Ritual.

Magic

Israel Regardie tells us (*The Golden Dawn* Vol. 3 P.9) that in their ritual, and doubtless based on tradition, that the apex of the pentagram was regarded as the point representing Spirit, and the other four points figured the Cherubim of Ezekiel, the Man or Angel, the Bull, the Lion, and the Eagle (representing the higher aspect of the Scorpion). That is Aquarius, Taurus, Leo and Aquilla (for Scorpio), which are the houses of the planets; saturn and the element Air, venus and Earth, sun and Fire, and for Scorpio, mars and Water; which are marked by the four Royal Stars of the Chaldeans, Formalhaut, Aldebaran, Regulus and Antares respectively.

When the pentagram is drawn by the magician's baton in the air, or when it is marked in a circle, it is visualised and marked with these four Cherubim in an anti-clockwise manner as they rise in the heavens. As there are five points in a pentagram instead of four as in a cross, these Cherubim, whose constellations are opposite each other in the heavens, and whose Royal Stars make a very nearly perfect cross in the sky, are placed on the points either side of the pentagram instead of at right angles. Aquarius and the Bull are generally placed on the left, and the Lion and Scorpion (or the Eagle) on the right. (See Fig. 14.)

If the Cherubim then represent the four quarters of the heavens, what does the apex stand for? Obviously the Pole Star in the north. This resembles our first pentagram with its apex to the North and Aquarius on its upper left point. The other constellations of the Cherubim do not fall on the points, but nevertheless we find that the Bull is on the left half and the Lion and Eagle (Scorpion) on the right. This is the pentagram of the moon and night when the planets and constellations are visible and all the stars seem to circle around the immovable Pole Star which because of this was thought to be the seat of the king of the gods in the heavens.

Since the constellations and houses of the Cherubim are those of Air, Earth, Fire and Water, the fifth is that of the Ether, element of Spirit and of course the Holy Spirit which is appropriately symbolised by the Pole Star.

Microcosmic Man

When we began to look for our first pentagram we mentioned the Microcosmic Man bound to the cross of form, or incarnation. He is bound by four nails, those of the elements Earth, Water, Air and Fire, just as Jesus was depicted as being fixed to the cross by four nails, however, in later times His feet were shown as crossed with only one nail driven in, making three in all. If we place the figure of a man in both the first and second pentagrams, the head at the apex and the arms in the upper angles and the feet in the lower, remembering that as he faces us the left side of the pentagram is the right side of his body, and conversely his left the right of the pentagram, we now see that:

	First Pentagram of Religion	**Second Pentagram of Church**
Right Hand	$341\frac{1}{2}°$ in Aquarius, saturn's day house	$159°$ in Leo, sun's day house
Right Foot	$51\frac{1}{2}°$ in Aries, mars' day house, sun exalted, saturn's fall	$236°$ in Libra, venus' day house, saturn exalted, sun's fall

The right side of a man's body (Pingala – of Yoga) is masculine, of the sun and day. Here in both pentagrams the planets are in accord all being in their day houses.

	First Pentagram of Religion	**Second Pentagram of Church**
Left Hand	192½° in Virgo, mercury's night house, mercury's exaltation, venus' fall	22° in Pisces, jupiter's night house, venus exalted, mercury's fall
Left Foot	123½° in Cancer, moon's night house, jupiter exalted, mars' fall	305° in Capricorn, saturn's night house, mars exalted, jupiter's fall

The left side of a man's body (Ida – of Yoga) is feminine, of the moon and night. We recall that the sun and moon have only one house each. Here also all the planets are in accord with his left side. The exaltations and falls are also interesting. (See Fig. 15.)

Microcosmic Woman

We will now place a person in the same manner in the third and fourth pentagrams which gives us:

	Third Pentagram of Pan & Fertility	**Fourth pentagram of Virgin Mary, Ceres & Harvest**
Right Hand	68° in Taurus, venus' night house, moon exalted	247° in Scorpio, mars' night house, moon's fall
Right Foot	139° in Cancer, moon's night house, jupiter exalted, mars' fall	321° in Capricorn, saturn's night house, mars exalted, jupiter's fall

Again all the planets are in their night houses, but you will note that this is the right side of this person's body. And again:

	Third Pentagram of Pan & Fertility	**Fourth pentagram of Virgin Mary, Ceres & Harvest**
Left Hand	284° in Sagittarius, jupiter's day house	108½° in Gemini, mercury's day house
Left Foot	213½° in Libra, venus' day house, saturn exalted, sun's fall	37½° in Aries, mars' day house, sun exalted, saturn's fall

Here the planets are all in their day houses, and it is the left side of the body, why? The answer to this mystery is that in a woman the sun is placed on the left side and the moon on the right, a fact that is little known, but quite apparent when you consider that a woman's nature tends to develop the opposite faculties to that of a man. (See Fig. 16.)

In these last two pentagrams facing East and West, their apex and vertical axis falls on the horizontal bar of our cross, that of the feminine, the world and matter. Here then we have

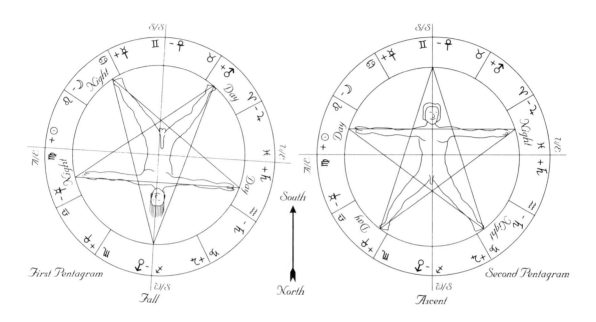

Fig. 15. Microcosmic Man.

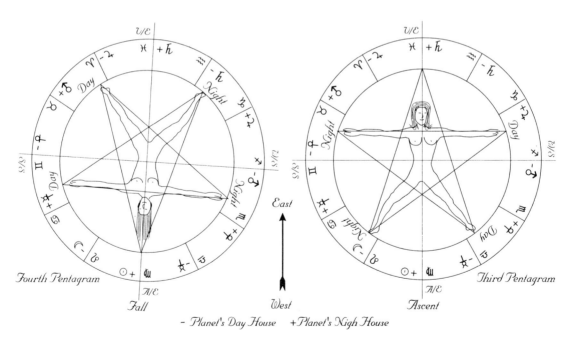

− Planet's Day House   + Planet's Nigh House

Fig. 16. Microcosmic Woman.

a female on the cross in the pentagram of the West and East, of Pan — fertility, Ceres — harvest. We have heard a lot about the Microcosmic Man, but I have never before read anything about the Microcosmic Woman. Have you?

Christ crucified on the cross is considered as the Second Adam, for when Adam was cast out of the garden of Eden we fell into sin and by Christ we are redeemed. Eve sinned as well and was cast forth with Adam, so the Microcosmic Woman is Eve, but who is the Second Eve? — the Virgin Mary!

We have associated her with Virgo, the place of the autumn equinox, and she wept at the foot of the cross at the crucifixion, which happened when the vernal equinox had just entered Pisces. Mr Owen Morgan informed us (*The Light of Britannia*) that in the Welsh almanacs down to his day, Lady Day (March 25th of the 'Annunciation') is called 'The day of the impregnation of Mary of the Equinoctial Line,' he considered it to be a Druidic survival, and referred to the Virgin Earth then being impregnated by the Sun God. Thus she was openly associated with the equinoxes (and the horizontal arms of our cross). She is also connected with the sea (Mare is the Latin for sea), which has the perfectly level horizon. I think that we can also include the other 'Marys', (so loved by the Celtic Church) under the concept of the Ascendant Microcosmic Woman.

The souls enter the world by the gate of the summer solstice, which is the place of the 'birth' of the moon (mind), where they identify themselves with the masculine vertical axis (spirit) of the cross. They then descend around the zodiac to the place of the autumn equinox on the feminine horizontal axis (matter), where they are separated into the two sexes.

This horizontal axis of the equinoxes divides the heavens into the upper and lower hemispheres. Subject to desire they 'fall' from the upper hemisphere in the summer half of the year to the lower one of winter, figuratively from Heaven to Hell.

When they reach the place of the winter solstice they are again in contact with the axis of spirit, the place of the 'birth' of the sun (heart) in the year. This helps them to rise, and they travel to the place of sacrifice at the vernal equinox where they cross over into the upper hemisphere and ascend to the place of the summer solstice. They are then embodied, having been fixed to the cross of the world and the year, and formed by the four pentagrams of the elements. They then go to their birth sign and begin to breath. In the Aries Era we had:

+ Masculine - Feminine	Sign + Day Sign - Night	Soul takes on Element of	Pentagram*
+ Summer solstice	♋ - ☽	Water	Third
- Autumn equinox	♎ + ♀	Air	Second
+ Winter solstice	♑ - ♄	Earth	Fourth
- Vernal equinox	♈ + ♂	Fire	First
But in the Piscean Era it is:			
+ Summer solstice	♊ + ☿	Air	Second
- Autumn equinox	♍ - ☿	Earth	Fourth
+ Winter solstice	♐ + ♃	Fire	First
- Vernal equinox	♓ - ♃	Water	Third

* The apex of each pentagram has the sign of the solstice or equinox for its Era.

The above shows that in the Aries Era it has the same order of the elements and planets as in the five day intercalary week, the exception being the Moon instead of Jupiter, both of which however are connected with the element of water. The fifth day of Mercury corresponds to the fifth pentagram of the Great Mother and ether.Most of this is given to us in the story of Adam and Eve in Genesis. Adam was an asexual being, created presumably at the summer solstice like all other embodied souls. He was in communion with God in the Garden of Eden (this here was the constellation of Cancer and the moon (mind), for the story appears to have been adapted for the Aries Era). He became lonely, so God put him into a deep sleep, and removed a 'rib' from his body from which he made Eve. If we look at the Microcosmic Man, we see that the feminine horizontal axis of the cross and equinoctial line cuts across his ribs. Why is one 'rib' only mentioned when there must have been two? presumably in order to emphasise the autumn equinox of the Fall where Eve the Microcosmic Woman 'fell' (is inverted).

Adam, infatuated by her beauty, was easily persuaded into 'disobedience' to the command of God, and ate the forbidden fruit with her. Having lost their innocence they were judged (Libra, the scales) by God, and expelled from the garden of Eden (Heaven, the upper hemisphere of summer) into the World (Hell, the lower hemisphere of winter) where they had to suffer and toil. They gave birth to Cain who became a 'tiller of the soil', and then to their second son Abel a 'shepherd'.

Cain was presumably a solar being (sun — heart) conceived at the winter solstice and born nine months later at the autumn equinox. Thus he offered to God the 'fruit of the earth' on his birthday at harvest time, which was the time of the 'fall', marked by Libra which in Chaldea was called the Holy Altar. His offering was not acceptable having sprung from the earth or lower hemisphere, to which he belonged.

Abel then was a lunar being (moon - mind) conceived at the summer solstice and born at the vernal equinox. His offerings of Paschal lambs at this time of Aries (the Ram), and the 'resurrection' of the sun, pleased God, for they and Abel belonged to the upper hemisphere. The new moon at the time of the equinoxes, were the two great festivals of the Chaldean and later the Jewish year. Cain was jealous and very angry, his heart overcoming his mind caused him to kill Abel. (The old moon which 'dies' and disappears from the night sky before it reappears as the new moon.)

This must have been just before the appearance of the new moon of the first month of the year, when the sun was in Aries (of Mars and Fire). Cain would have thus made a blood offering to the Great Earth Mother, for the ancients made blood Sacrifices and this was poured on the ground or into 'trenches' for the gods of the underworld. The gods of heaven such as the Olympic gods were given Burnt Offerings, which rose as smoke into the sky, and Aries the Ram being burnt up by the sun's rays at the spring equinox was the archetype of the latter.

V   Surrounding Churches

We will now look at the churches and châteaux of the towns and villages of the surrounding region and see what alignments they make with our Cross. We will note the corresponding saints' days, limiting them to the end of the sixth century to agree with the period of our Cross, similarly we will list only the churches and châteaux which were contemporary.

Church/Château	Position	Date	Saint
Granès	20½°	11 March 12 March	St Pionius 250 AD St Constantine King of the Scots, monk and arch-martyr of Scotland. Phinehas High Priest of Israel.
Quillan	27°	18 March (17 March	Alexander bishop of Jerusalem, martyr. St Patrick.)
Le Bézu	51½°	11 April 12 April (10 April	St Antipas. Sabas the Goth. St Leo the Great. Ezekiel.)
Bugarach	139°	12 July	St Hermagoras.
Sougraigne	176½°	19 August 20 August	'The Apparition of the Cross'. Samuel. St Amator.
Arques (church) Arques (château)	234° 238°	17 October 21 October	St Florentius, patron of Orange. 524 AD. St Hilarion. St Ursula and virgins.
(Peyro Dreto)	249½°	1 November 2 November	All Saints. All Souls.
Serres (church) Serres (château)	268½° 270°	21 November 22 November	Presentation of the BVM. St Caecilia. Northern arm of cross.
Peyrolles	277°	29 November	St Saturnin.
Cassaignes	296°	17 December	St Lazarus.
Luc sur Aude	311½°	1-2 January	
Coustaussa	318°	8 January	
Couiza	330°	20 January	St Fabian. St Sebastian. The sun enters Aquarius.
Espéraza	347°	6/7 February	

If we continue the northern arm of our cross from the Devil's Chair we find that it exactly passes through the Château of Serres, now according to Louis Fédié (*Comte de Razés* p.147) this noble's manor was built on the ruins of a Visigothic fort which was later destroyed by the Saracens.

It is also interesting to observe that the church of Peyrolles which is situated to the West of the village, is within $1^1/3°$ from the true northern axis of our cross.

The Visigoths

As our cross was apparently aligned by the Visigoths, let us briefly recall their history in the region. When their leader Atawulf married the Roman Princess Galla Placidia in 414 AD, he received as dowry the lands of Provincia and Septimania. They made the ancient city of Toulouse their capital, which was said to have been founded by a legendary king called Aquarius. Saturn has his planet's day house in the sign of Aquarius, and perhaps this is why its first bishop and Patron saint who was martyred there in 250 AD was called St Saturnin (now shortened to Sernin). Because he refused to sacrifice to their idols, the pagans of Toulouse tied Saturnin with a rope to the tail of a bull and lashed the animal so that it ran down a hill, and in so doing, dashed out the saint's brains on the rocks.

Toulouse fell to the Franks in 507 AD, so the Visigoths removed their capital to Toledo in Spain. They then fortified the area around Rennes le Château and Rennes les Bains, the ancient town of Rhedae was somewhere within this perimeter, and it was to here that they withdrew.

The alignment from the Cross to the church at Peyrolles gives the festival of St Saturnin in the calendar, but remarkably enough the church is dedicated to this same saint, also the alignment to Couiza falls on the 20th of January, when the sun enters the sign of Aquarius, the middle of the intercalary days in our Drudic Year; which recalls King Aquarius. Thus they have retained the memory and blessings of the patron and founder of their capital Toulouse. I think that this, as well as the Château of Serres alignment is very convincing proof of the genuine antiquity of our cross.

Le Peyro Dreto Menhir (Pierre Dressée)

The stream of Peyrolles on which the village of the same name is situated joins the River Rialsesse a little to the West of this menhir, which is situated on the hillside above the road to Arques, this is very important, as it is the only megalith accepted as unquestionably genuine in the region. The Abbé Ancé in 1900 observed that it leans to the South-South-West, which is of course an approximation. South-South-West is $22^1/2°$ West of true South, and is therefore roughly 14° West of the southern axis of our Cross.

This aligns in the calendar with the 7th of May, the feast of St Raphael the archangel, Origen calls him 'the Angel to whom the work of healing is committed', most appropriate to our Holy Valley. The word 'Peyrolles' comes from the Occitan *Peire Ola* meaning 'stone urn' or 'funeral stone', which is what menhirs were often thought to be in the middle ages.

This confirms the conjecture which has been made about this stone being connected with the origin of the name of the river and village. Now what is amazing, is that it aligns with our cross at $249^1/2°$ which falls between the 1st, All Saints Day, and the 2nd of November All

The Menhir (Le Peyro Dreto).

Souls Day, when the dead were remembered. The 1st was the beginning of the Celtic New Year and called Samhain or Samhuin which meant the 'season of peace', it was deliberately misnamed by the early Christians, who called it Allhallow implying hallowed to the saints, when really it should be All heal as its name comes from *Uil-ic*, (mistletoe) the all-healer or universal remedy. This is very appropriate to our Valley of the Cross with its 'healing' hot baths and mineral waters.

Arques Church. 17th of October

Here is a remarkable alignment, Arques (Archae, Archas) of course suggests the Ark, as the French word *arquer* (Latin *Arcuo*) to 'bend', to 'arch'; and *arche* (Latin *Arca*) 'chest' or 'box' — the Ark (of Noah). Now to suggest that this refers to Noah's Ark may sound farfetched and yet amazingly enough, even though it may have been a 'double-entendre', it does.

The Babylonian and Jewish months began with the month Nisan and this began with the new moon around the vernal equinox, an intercalary month having occasionally to be inserted so that this was never more than one month either side of it. For simplicity, the Jewish months have often been taken to coincide with ours, thus Nisan with April. (Usually taken as mid-month. These lunar months were judged from the sighting of the new moon, and rarely agreed with the solar ones).

The Ark grounded on mount Ararat on the 17th of the 7th month, that of Tishri in our October. So here we have it, Arques Church commemorates the grounding of the Ark, and its alignment from the centre of our cross cuts through the hill above Arques called La Berco Grando. (The pronunciation of the vowels like A and E here often varied in local dialects, and unlike the consonants, the spelling often differed.) Could this be a corruption of the Latin word *Barca*, from which is derived our word 'Bark', and the French *Barque*? Then the Big Bark (La Berco Grando) would be Noah's large Ark, and it is not unreasonable to suggest that the Little Bark (La Berco Petito), the hill alongside which happens to be about the same size and height, refers to the little boat that brought the Virgin Mary and her companions to Marseilles.

Arques Fairs

Albert Fabre in his *History of Arques* p.23 says, 'Arques has two fairs, that of the 26th of July and of the 20th of October'. At the first are shown all sorts of industrial products,, 'at that of the 18th of October one brings there also the porcine race'. In a footnote he says, 'The fair of the 20th of October is of recent creation.' I take this to mean that originally one fair was held on the 26th of July the festival of 'The falling asleep of St Anne, mother of the Virgin Mary', Patron of Arques Church (also dedicated to St John the Baptist), whose name suggests the ancient Celtic goddess Anu; and the other on the 18th of October. The fact that the latter is associated with pigs which were sacred to the ancient Gauls and Celts in general, implies that it has come down to us from Pagan times, as is customary with the majority of, if not all old fairs. It is most interesting to see that this fair is held on the morrow of that given by our alignment to Arques Church, and might have lasted originally for four days from the 17th to the 20th of October.

Cassaignes (may be from the Gaulish word Cassano an oak)

Our alignment to the church falls on the 17th of December the festival of St Lazarus, who Jesus 'raised' from the dead. Once again the number 17 is present. According to the tradition of the Celtic Church Lazarus with his sisters Martha and Mary came with the Virgin Mary to Gaul. He was very important symbolically, as the first Christian fish drawn out of the sea of existence into the Life Immortal of which Jesus preached. So here we have the Druid's Tree of Life. The oak is resurrected.

Sougraigne

> 19th of August. 'The Apparition of the Cross'
> 20th of August. Samuel, prophet. St Amator servant of the Virgin Mary

Here we have the memorial of the Apparition of the Cross to the Emperor Constantine, which was of such importance to the early Christian Church. Samuel was the last of the succession of Judges of Israel, who founded the Kingship by anointing Saul and perhaps also David, this locally would seem to indicate the Arch-Druid in our valley anointing the future king of the local tribe, probably seated on a sacred stone near the present Devil's Chair.

86

In the time that the local druids were converted to Christianity, the bishop would have superseded the pagan high priest. St Amator was the servant of the Virgin Mary and sailed to Gaul with her, he retired from the world and lived as a hermit *(Chronicon Roberti de Monte)* and was associated with Roch Amadour a mountain solitude in Quercy (presumably from the Latin *Quercus* an oak, thus a Christianised Druidic Holy Place), which was a famous place of pilgrimage in the middle ages. Here again the Celtic Church tradition is recorded in this alignment.

Bugarach

Here is St Hermagoras the disciple of St Mark (12 July). This name is derived from Hermes, god of travellers, and is suitable as the road from the valley to the South leads through the village of Bugarach.

Le Bézu

This important alignment falls between the 11th and 12th of April, the 11th is the day of St Leo the Great who risked his life in interceding with Attila, King of the Huns, and persuaded him not to attack Rome. On the 12th we have St Sabas the Goth, a martyr; and on the eve of our alignment, (the 10th) the prophet Ezekiel.

Quillan

Here on the 18th of March we have the blessed Alexander bishop of Jerusalem martyred in 251 AD, the eve is the festival of St Patrick (464 AD).

Granès

I am uncertain as to the age of this village, whose name however possibly comes from Grian, a name of the Celtic sun god personified. This aligns with St Pionius and his companions who were early martyrs, and the later St Constantine, King of the Scots, their chief martyr who died in 576 AD, it also covers the 12th of March, the alignment falling between the 11th and 12th, which is the memorial of Phinehas a high priest of Israel and grandson of Aaron, whose presence suggests the memory of the Druidical priests of our 'Cromleck' or circle.

Rennes les Bains showing the bridge that was washed away by recent floods. (Postcard before 1900.)

Quillan, with the old stone bridge over the Aude. (Postcard before 1900.)

We will now put the signs of the zodiac clockwise around our Cross. Keeping the 0° on the western arm we will now have 90° on the northern and 270° on the southern arm, the eastern arm being at 180° as before.

Instead of starting the signs from the western arm with the beginning of Pisces, we will now align the northern arm of the cross 90° with the 30th of July in the calendar. This is in order to align the church of Serres with its saint's day, that of St Peter in chains and Lammas (Lugnasad). We will put the signs around the cross as before, but as the 30th of July is seven days into Leo likewise we will put the other arms seven days into their signs. We now have:

The Sun Enters	Date	Plus 7 Days	Saint	Arm of Cross
Taurus	20 April	27th April (28 April	St Theodore. St Vitalis.)	0°
Leo	23 July	(29th July	St Martha.)	90°
Scorpio	23 October	30 October	St Marcellus. Dedication of King Solomon's Temple.	180°
Aquarius	20 January	27 January	St Chrysostom.	270°

Our Cross here marks the octave of the sun's entry into the four fixed signs of the zodiac. Here are the four Cherubim allotted to the four Evangelists, the Bull (Taurus) of St Luke, the Lion (Leo) of St Mark, the Eagle (Aquila) above the Scorpion (Scorpio) of St John, and the Water Carrier (Aquarius) the Man of St Matthew. We now get the following:

Church/Château	Position	Date	Saint
Espéraza	13°	10 May (11 May	Job, prophet. St Mamertus.)
Couiza	30°	28 May	St Theodulos Stylites of the pillar.
Coustaussa	42°	9 June	St Columba. 597 AD.
Luc sur Aude	48½°	15 June 16 June	— St Quiricus.
Cassaignes	64°	2 July	—
Peyrolles	83°	23 July (22 July	St Apollinaris, 1st bishop of Ravenna, martyr. 74 AD. St Mary Magdalen.)
Serres (château) Serres (church)	90° 91½°	(29 July 30 July 31 July 1 August	St Martha.) Northern arm of our cross. St Germanus, bishop of Auxerre. 448 AD. St Peter in chains, Lammas.
(Peyro Dreto)	110½°	20 August	Samuel, prophet. St Amator.

89

Church/Château	Position	Date	Saint
Arques (château)	122°	1 September	St Anna, prophetess who honoured the infant Jesus in the Temple.
Arques (church)	126°	5 September	St Onesiphorus, martyr, friend of St Paul.
Sougraigne	183½°	2 November	All Souls.
Bugarach	221°	9 December	St Leocadia.
le Bézu	308½°	6 March 7 March	— SS Perpetua and Felicitas, martyrs. 203 AD.
Quillan	333°	31 March (1 April	— Memorial of Adam.)
Granès	339½°	6 April 7 April	Beginning of our Lord's preaching. St Hegesippus, ancient Father of the Church. 180 AD.

We see that the memorial of St Apollinaris falls on the alignment of Peyrolles which had previously agreed with its dedication to St Saturnin of such local importance. St Apollinaris of Antioch who had been ordained by St Peter, and as the first bishop of Ravenna, is clearly very important to the Visigoths of our Valley because of its connection with Galla Placidia whose story we shall shortly come to, also the eve is the day of St Mary Magdalen to whom the church of Rennes le Château is dedicated, a 'star' of the Celtic Church.

It is also remarkable that the prophet Samuel is present (who we compared to the Arch Druid), and also St Amator, both of whom are now indicated by that venerable menhir the Peyro Dreto. Furthermore, All Souls which it previously marked; is now shown by Sougraigne Church. At Arques château we have St Anna the elderly prophetess who spent all her time in the temple and who recognised the future greatness of the infant Jesus. A fair was held at Arques on the day of the grandmother of Jesus, St Anne who is the patron of its church. SS Anna and Anne have obviously replaced the worship of the Celtic Great Mother goddess Anu or Ana which we will come to later.

Quillan has the Memorial of Adam or the 'first man', and this is followed by that of Granès (if this church existed) of the Beginning of the Lord's preaching, here signifying the coming of Christianity to the valley and the region of the Druids.

The alignment to Luc sur Aude, that falls on the day of St Quiricus seems to refer to the Druids, as his name is obviously derived from *Quercus* Latin for a common oak, their sacred tree.

Espéraza here commemorates Job the prophet on the 10th of May, and on the morrow we have St Mamertus of whom we shall have more to say later.

Arms of the Cross

The western arm now falls on the 27th of April, day of St Theodore abbot of Tabenne in Egypt (367 AD). The morrow is that of St Vitalis patron of Ravenna. The northern arm marks the 30th of July for which I cannot find any relevant saint, the previous day however

90

is that of St Martha sister of Mary and Lazarus, and the morrow, that of St Germanus of Auxerre who died at Ravenna. He was warmly welcomed there by the Empress Galla Placidia who was very devoted to him. This is important as is the presence of St Vitalis, patron of Ravenna, for as we will see shortly, she appears to have visited and been very impressed by our Valley.

The eastern arm marks the 30th of October, the day of the dedication of King Solomon's Temple, and that of St Marcellus which previously aligned with Montferrand château, so relevant to the Valley. This Alternative Arrangement of our Cross is set to agree with the dedication of the Church of Serres, on which falls the festival of Lugnasad, the Christian Lammas. The Celtic festival of Lugnasad was connected with the sun god Lug's ritual marriage, which was held chiefly in honour of the dead ancestors, and was called 'the Wedding of Kingship' for Nassad implies tying or binding together.

These were the nuptials of the sun as the Sky Father with the Earth Mother, and consequently a popular time for marriages. Thus we see in a different context the 'binding' of St Peter in chains, and his miraculous escape from prison commemorated on this day, however I cannot help thinking that the Arian Visigoths saw in this a limitation to the power and claims of the Bishop of Rome.

Discovery

Sougraigne Church is dedicated to the 'Invention de St Étienne (415 AD). As we have seen how it represented 'The Apparition of the Cross to Constantine', the prophet Samuel and All Souls Day in our alignments. St Stephen (Étienne in French) was the first Christian martyr, and his suffering was witnessed by St Paul. The priest Lucian, following the inspiration of a dream in 415 AD found the unknown burial place of St Stephen, and with him in the same sepulchre lay Nicodemus, Gamaliel, and his son Abibas. In our context this dedication to the 'Finding of St Stephen' seems to indicate that we need to discover the four arms of the cross in the valley of Rennes les Bains. These four men in a Cabalistic way symbolise the four arms of the cross, in the same manner as SS Anthony, Mary Magdalene, Roch and Germaine do in the church of Rennes le Château.

The Roman Princess and the Cross

Galla Placidia, daughter of the first baptised Christian Emperor Theodosius the Great, was taken prisoner by Alaric King of the Visigoths during the siege of Rome in 41 AD. In the same year Alaric died and was succeeded by his brother-in-law Atawulf who decided that it would be better to make peace with the Romans, therefore, with the consent of the Roman Emperor her half brother, he married Galla Placidia and received as a dowry Provincia (Provence) and Septimania (Languedoc). The marriage took place with great pomp and ceremony at Narbonne on Thursday 1st of January 414 AD, but unfortunately Atawulf was murdered by his groom at Barcelona in the following year, and Wallia became king.

On Monday 1st of January 417 AD she married Constantius, (after having been released by the Visigoths in 416 AD). On the death of the Emperor Honorius in 421 AD, she moved

Mausoleum of Galla Placidia, Ravenna. (Postcard.)

from their home in Constantinople to Ravenna, then she reigned there with her son Valentinian III, who was proclaimed Emperor in 423 AD when he was only six, and she died in 450 AD. In her time the cross, as a sign, became widely revered, but it is important to emphasise that no crucifix as such was known in the first seven centuries AD.

The Rev W W Seymour in *The Cross in Traditional History and Art* p.157 says: 'that to her [Galla Placidia] we are indebted for the first instance that can be authenticated of the cross occupying a prominent position in large monuments of art. Her sepulchral chapel is in the church of SS Nazairo e Celso built in 440 AD at Ravenna; the dome is azure with golden stars, in the midst of which shines a golden cross" (Quoting from *History of Our Lord* by Mrs Jameson and Lady Eastlake v.2 p.138.)

This chapel is dedicated to St Laurence (258 AD) and known as the 'guardian of the Treasures of the Church' because although he was entrusted with them by his bishop, he preferred to distribute them to the poor rather than hand them over to the Persecutors of the Christians, and was martyred. The chapel is in the shape of a Greek cross which was built on the south side of the narthex of the main church with another identical one on the north side. The church itself which has been demolished, was also of a cruciform shape, and therefore has been called St Croce. In the chapel of St Laurence, unlike the other churches at Ravenna, in order to emphasise the cross surrounded by the Cherubim, all the Apostles

Cross at the centre of the mosaic ceiling in the dome of the Mausoleum of Galla Placidia.

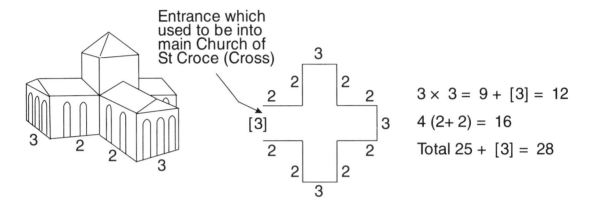

Fig. 17. Saints Nazairo e Celso Chapel, Ravenna.

depicted in mosaic around the walls look up to the Latin cross in the dome. The outside of the chapel is decorated with three blind arches on each wall end of the arms of the cross, and two on either side of the arms. One of these arms however is open, for that is where the chapel joined the main church, and today it is its entrance. Thus we have in the three end walls of the cross shaped chapel nine blind arches, and in the eight sides sixteen other blind arches, totalling twenty five in all. If we add to this three more, for the side where the chapel was joined to the church, we have twenty eight the number of the mansions of the moon.

Similarly the golden cross depicted in the dome is surrounded by 570 golden stars. This number is 19×30 or $19 \times 10 \times 3$, the 19 years of the metonic cycle and the 30 days of the month; or does 3 stand for the Trinity, 10 for Jehovah, the Old and New Testaments and the 19 year cycle? Also by theosophical arithmetic $5 + 7 + 0 = 12$ the number of the months, Apostles, etc. clearly the zodiac and the year have been deliberately associated here with the cross.

Now the church at Rennes les Bains is also dedicated to SS Nazaire et Celse. They were particularly dear to the Celtic Church as St Celse was born at Cimiez near Nice, and it was customary in the martyrologies of the early church to remember mainly their local saints.

The Valley with its thermal springs and sources so sacred to the pagan Celts was evidently a Temple, and after their conversion to Christianity, these ancient Druids carried on their newly adopted religion in this natural open air shrine.

When Galla Placidia was married to Atawulf at Narbonne, and lived in this Visigothic kingdom as its queen for nearly three years, she must surely have visited Rennes les Bains the Spa which had been so popular with the Romans. Undoubtedly she was told about the history of the Valley, and its Cross in the heavens of the zodiac, formed by the solstices and the equinoxes, though we do not know whether at this time there was one laid out in the valley below.

She was surely also reminded of her great predecessor the Emperor Constantine who saw the Gallic Chi-Rho Cross in the sky above the sun, which he adopted as his ensign, and his British mother who discovered the True Cross at Jerusalem. Did she see the midnight sky around the time of the summer solstice when Jupiter's Eagle and that of St John, Aquila, was

94

nearly at the zenith, because at this latitude Cygna the swan would then have been right overhead, its main stars alpha, beta, gamma, delta and epsilon form a little Latin cross which apparently she remembered and placed in the centre of the dome of her chapel at Ravenna, for the same phenomenon occurred there as it is only $1^1/2°$ of latitude North of Rennes les Bains. Doubtless it was called by the Gauls, the Goose, after their sacred bird, for in old Irish a swan was *Geis* which is cognate with the English Geese.

There is another phenomenon at this latitude of Rennes les Bains 42° 55′ and at Ravenna latitude 44° 26′ of which I am sure they told her, as it would have been of great interest to the Druids and their Christian converts, bearing in mind how fascinated they were with Triads of all sorts. The path of the ecliptic on which the sun appears to travel across the sky crosses the celestial equator at the equinoxes, and therefore has the same declination. The greatest angle that the ecliptic makes with the equator is $23^1/2°$. Thus at midday on the meridian at the summer solstice, looking due South we see the sun $23^1/2°$ higher in the sky than at the equinoxes; similarly at the winter solstice it is $23^1/2°$ lower.

Latitude is measured on the globe from the equator to the pole, so a latitude of 43° is 47° from the pole. If the horizon is level ground, then that of the equator on the meridian is the same angle as the pole to the zenith of the observer. So at latitude 43° the sun at midday on the winter solstice being $23^1/2°$ below the equator, is therefore $23^1/2°$ above the horizon. At the summer solstice it is $23^1/2°$ above the equator, so at this latitude the position of the sun at the solstices and equinoxes divides the meridian exactly into three equal parts of $23^1/2°$.

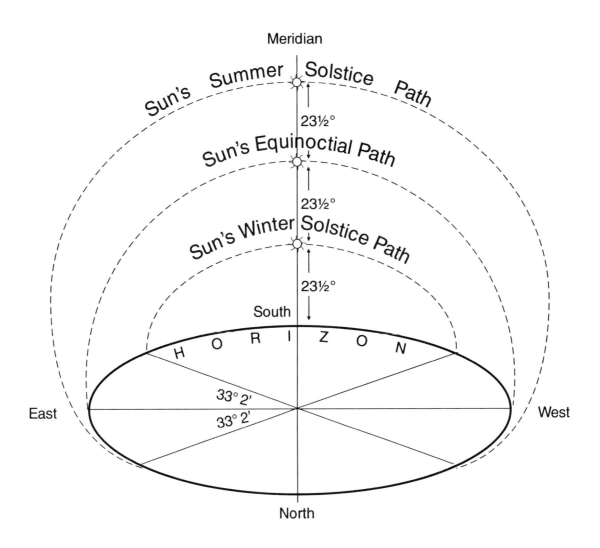

Fig. 18. Sun's path at Latitude 43 degrees.

VI   History

Inspiration

Did the local people tell their new Queen Placidia about the Druidic Year, with its two halves ending on the day of St Anthony the Hermit? This would have been very interesting to her, for did not her father the Emperor Theodosius die of dropsy at Milan on Wednesday the 17th of January 395 AD? or was this given date contrived to fit the end of this year?

We can be sure that when she stayed at the spa of Rennes les Bains the christianised Druids* explained many of these astral mysteries to her and inspired her with the enthusiasm which, when she came into a position of power as regent at Ravenna, she was able to express in her own mortuary chapel. She even named it after the Gallic St Celse (who is not mentioned in the Liturgical Year of Rome), and his companion St Nazaire, and I think it most probable that there was a little church before the present one dedicated at that time to St Nazaire and Celse.

We have seen how the Cross in our Holy Valley probably dates from around 451 AD. (448 + 3 the possible error in estimation). It was very likely that the laying out of our Cross was suggested by Galla Placidia herself when she was staying at Narbonne, for we know how impressed she was by the Latin Cross, and as we have already seen she was the first to propagate it 'in a prominent position in large monuments of art' as the sign of Christ. We have surmised that she was inspired by what the Christian druids told her about the little cross of stars that make up the constellation Cygnus when she visited the Holy Valley of Rennes les Bains.

This then is one of the great secrets of our valley, how it played its part in promoting the Christian Latin cross in preference to the Chi-Rho cross of Constantine and the Gauls, and is well supported by the fact that the Visigoths, long after Galla Placidia had left the region, had great respect for Rhedae and the valley; for as we have seen, they clearly laid out the Cross, marking it with alignments to their forts at Serres, Blanchefort and Montferrand.

The Cross, by its alignments and the correspondence with the calendar gives some amazing 'coincidences' which I have pointed out, and it is also clear from its association with Mary Magdalen, Martha, Lazarus, and many other saints especially beloved by the Celtic Church, that it was designed with their full support. The Church in Languedoc and Provence

---

*   In this book I use the term Druid loosely to cover most of the pagan Celtic priests, but Julius Cæsar called only those of the Belgae Druids, which tribe never occupied the region of Rhedae. Doubtless they learnt a lot from the traditions of the earlier peoples priests in Gaul and Britain, which may have been passed down from the Megalithic builders.

apparently got on much better with their Arian Christian overlords the Visigoths, than is recorded in the propaganda of the later pro-Roman historians. With regard to Rome, Pope Zosimus (417 - 18) attempted to form a papal Vicarite at Arles over the Viennensis and the two Narbonenses which did not succeed, and afterwards the See at Rome gave up such obvious empire building, later popes often appointed well known Gallic and Spanish bishops to represent them personally and only as intermediaries. The popes, nonetheless were held in great respect, and their doctrinal decisions were mostly accepted.

The Celtic Church

I have used the term Celtic Church instead of Gallic Church to refer to the Christians in the south of France. I have done this deliberately, as otherwise one forgets that the Church in Gaul and that in Britain were sister churches of the same family, having as their common tradition the fact that they were founded by St Joseph of Arimathea when he came by boat to Marseilles with the Virgin Mary, Mary Magdalen, Martha and Lazarus, Mary Cleophas, Mary Salome, Maximen, Cleon, Trophimus, Saturnin, Martilla, Sedony, Eutrope and Martial.

Druidic Background

It is well known that the Druids on the continent had a great respect for the British Druids, for they were a centre of pure druidic tradition and ancient knowledge. They were therefore often visited by their brothers from the mainland, for this reason it was much easier for the early British Church to convert the continent than for missionaries from elsewhere. Rome for example was for them the hated centre of the conquerors who had destroyed their Druid priests, and with them their culture. True it had brought peace and prosperity, trade and a different civilisation, but nevertheless they were subject to a foreign power.

Doubtless there were still some covert Druids in existence, and of course much of what we refer to as pagan rites and customs preserved this tradition, or at least the practises, their dogma was mainly lost to history. So British (and later Irish) Christian priests spread the Gospel over most of neighbouring Europe, to Switzerland and even to northern Italy. It was very prestigious for them to be able to claim both St Helena and her father King Cole of Colchester as Christians, and she was also of course the mother of the Emperor Constantine, who established Christianity as the religion of the Roman empire. When later she became a Roman Empress, she was reputed to have found the true Cross of Christ at Jerusalem which added to her glory.

However the most important thing was the tradition that St Joseph of Arimathea came with the Virgin Mary and 12 disciples and settled in Glastonbury, where she, and later St Joseph, were buried in the Aulde Kirk, a building of mud and wattle, which was the way of the Celts. This was covered with lead in the time of the Saxon conquest to preserve it, but unfortunately later burnt to the ground in an accident.

This was the oldest above ground church in the world that we know about, and the first dedicated to the Mother of Jesus. There are two different dates for the founding of this church. Gildas the Wise the earliest Christian historian informed us that the 'Light of Christ' shone here in the last year of the reign of Tiberius Caesar (37 AD). Freculphus bishop of Lisieux in the 9th century (as quoted by William of Malmesbury) said that St Philip the apostle came to France from where he sent Joseph of Arimathea to Britain in 63 AD. St John, to whom Jesus handed over the protection of his mother, was therefore called her Paranymphos, which means attendant. St Joseph also received the same title as her attendant and is stated to have been present at her assumption. That provides a strong argument for the veracity of this story. The alternative version is as follows:

In the 4th century the Gnostics started a legend that St Mary lived on in Bethlehem after the crucifixion until an angel came and told her that her death was nigh, and carried her in a cloud to Jerusalem. The Apostles then took her to Gethsemane where the Archangel Gabriel received her soul and carried it to Paradise, whilst the Apostles transported her body to the valley of Jehosaphat and laid it in a tomb, then Christ appeared and told St Michael to collect her soul from Paradise, and re-unite it with her body, whereupon the angels carried it up to heaven.

This fable was denounced by St Epiphanius (bishop and theologian of Constantia in Cyprus (315 - 403 AD) who said: "The whole thing is foolish and strange, and is a device and deceit of the devil", the saintly Pope Gelasius condemned it (*De Transitu Virginis Mariae liber*) as heretical in 494 AD. Despite this the Emperor Maurice instituted the Festival of the Assumption in the 7th century, it was rejected by Charlemagne but accepted by his son Lewis, in 818 AD.

Which story seems the more reasonable, the tradition of the Celtic Church, or that adopted by the Roman? The successors of St Joseph and his companions lived separately as anchorites at the foot of the Tor, and when one of the 12 died another was appointed. Then later on, St Patrick (395 - 472 AD) founded the monastery, and was closely connected with it, however, it was not St Patrick, but St Joseph to whose memory the monks there fondly clung, thereby giving weight to the tradition.

Why have we no mention at all in the accepted chronicles of the time, such as *The Anglo Saxon Chronicle*, Bede's *Ecclesiastical History*, or the *Chronicle* of Fabius Ethelwerd? Clearly not because they did not know about Glastonbury but rather because they were neither Britons nor members of the Celtic Church, but foreigners writing for the Saxons who had been converted by the Roman Catholic church. They wrote after the advent of St Augustine in 597 who asked for submission to the Pope of Rome, and deliberately kept silent as they did not wish to mention a British Catholic Foundation which was older than that of Rome.

I think there is another explanation for the lack of written evidence, and this is that the pagan Celts and their priests the Druids, like most ancient peoples, learned by heart their history and religion, which practice was carried on until they came under the power of Rome, when the monastic scribes began to record these things. There is no doubt whatsoever that the Christian Church existed in Britain in the latter half of the second century, Tertullion (208 AD) said of the Britons who were in revolt against Severus that they were 'inaccessible to the Romans but subject to Christ' (Adv. Judaeos VII). Origen (239 AD) said: "notwithstanding the isolated situation of Britain, it [the Gospel] had penetrated even to that country" (Homil VI in Luc. 1 24).

Another argument in favour of the idea that the monks sincerely believed that St Joseph was buried at Glastonbury was that the list given in *The Monasticum* of relics kept at the abbey included fantastic things such as a lock of Jesus' hair, some teeth of St Peter, etc. but not a single relic of Joseph is mentioned. A known fact is that no relics are claimed of a Saint if his body was entire and the place of his burial known. The old church dedicated by St Joseph to the Virgin Mary (Cressy bk.2 ch.7) soon came to be known as St Joseph's chapel, which could never have happened if the early converts had not had very good grounds for believing that he had actually lived there; for it was the custom of the British Church to always name a church after its founder.

I am indebted to the Rev Lionel S Lewis and Walter Clifford Meller for most of the arguments and information given here.

The policy of the Roman Church was to convert the heathen conquerors, who would then force the Christians of other Rites to transfer their allegiance to the Pope of Rome, causing a bitter struggle with the Celtic Church, involving all sorts of political intrigue. Through the conversion of the Saxon kings they seized control of the Celtic Church in most of Britain, Glastonbury was handed over to Rome by King Ine of Wessex around 725 AD and was placed under the control of the monastery of Whithorn.

In the 8th century, the Emperor Charlemagne brought the rest of France, Saxony, Bavaria and Lombardy under the religious jurisdiction of Rome, and in the Isle of Man too, the Roman priests converted the heathen Vikings and thereby gained control of the local Culdee Church. Always and everywhere the same cunning strategy, a particularly bitter pill for the local Christians (who had been victimized for their belief by the same overlords before their sudden conversion to Christianity) to swallow.

The peoples of the Celtic Church, having such a wonderful tradition, despite being brought forcibly under Roman allegiance, continued the struggle to keep their traditions alive. Under Charlcmagne their Gallic Rite was suppressed in favour of the Roman one, and similarly about the same time, the British Rite was abolished, nevertheless the struggle went on until the Normans conquered England and put priests of their own blood to oversee the monasteries and Bishoprics.

About 200 years later, the Roman Catholics pursued their wicked campaign against the Cathars in the South of France, and later still against the Huguenots. They had devised the devilish institution of The Holy Inquisition, which delighted in the most inhumane tortures to gain admissions of guilt, and the roasting alive of all dissenters. This was in complete contrast to the teachings of Our Lord, in whose name they did these horrors, no wonder it was forbidden to translate the Holy Gospel into the local tongues. Unrepentant, though powerless, Rome still maintains this magnificent Christian institution.

Everything was done to suppress our Celtic Church. Where are the churches in France dedicated to its leader the Paranymphos St Joseph of Arimathea? This saint's day was left out of the Roman calendar so as to erase its connection with the Celtic Church. This is but another proof of their secret acknowledgement of the veracity of the claim of the Celtic Church of Britain to predate that of the Roman one, which has come down to us through such manuscripts as the Welsh story of the arrival of St Joseph by Maelgwynn of Landaff in the 3rd century.

When the British Bishops attended the early church Councils at Nicaea in 325 and 787 AD, they claimed precedence because of the priority of the church in Britain, similarly, Queen Elizabeth also claimed precedence, quoting her father's claim that 'Joseph of Arimathea planted Christian Religion immediately after the Passion of Christ in the Realme', in fact from Henry IV's reign to that of Charles I, for a period of 233 years, the Glastonbury Tradition was the basis of great national claims.

The historian and Benedictine monk Cressy, who was well versed in the treasured traditions of that great Benedictine monastery of Glastonbury, recorded that St Joseph of Arimathea died at Glastonbury on the 27th of July 82 AD. In Liège, which claims to hold

100

relics of St Joseph, he is fêted on the 22nd of February (the original date of St Peter's Chair, and on which British Bishops were consecrated) but it was at first held on the day of his death. The Greek Church kept his festival on the 31st, and at Glastonbury for the first six days of August, presumably this was in order to commemorate it on the important Celtic festival of Lugnasad, the Christian Lammas.

So here it is: on the day after the original date of his memorial is that of SS Nazaire and Celse. No wonder their fête was popular, for as well as at Rennes les Bains and Carcassonne, the Cathedral at Béziers is dedicated to them and also the old church at Foix of the 5th century or earlier, then in existence (for it received the martyred remains of St Volusien). Thus in defiance of the Roman Church which wished to banish the wonderful tradition of the Leader of the Celtic Church, his memory was kept alive.

Because the leader of the Celtic Church was the Paranymphos of the Virgin Mary, it was the first to honour her with a festival, especially in the countries of the Gallican Rite. Gregory of Tours (6th century) states that her festival was held in Gaul in the middle of January, and in the Hieran Martyrology of Gaul it is assigned to the 18th of January, the same day as that of St Peter's Chair.

The Celtic Church in Britain claimed that it was first established as an offshoot of the Coptic Church which at that time recognised the Syriac Church as the Mother Church of all Christendom, there St Peter was Bishop of Antioch before he became Bishop of Rome where the followers of Christ were first called Christians. (Acts XI 26) This old tradition claimed St Aristobulus, father-in-law to St Peter as first Bishop of Britain (recorded in the Greek menology). St Joseph was regarded as having been sent to Britain by St Mark, founder of the Coptic Church.

St Mary Magdalene was a particular favourite of the Celtic Church, and the first written mention of her festival was in the *British Martyrology* of Bede (673 - 735), later appearing in a Missal of Verona of the 10th century and in some of the 11th century missals but was not received into the official Roman books until the 13th century.

St Nazaire and Celse

The names of these saints may have been chosen for the local church because they seem to convey the 'Secret of the Valley'. In Gaelic *Cill* or *Ceal* (pronounced Keel as also *Celse* would have been *Kelse*) means 'heaven' or 'sky', and hence figuratively anything circular, this is synonymous with the Greek *Coilon* and Latin *Coelum* and could be the radic of both. Cill was the most appropriate and usual word for a Druidic temple and occurs everywhere. We can therefore take St Celsius as the same as the Latin *celsus* meaning 'high' or 'lofty'. St Nazaire, *Nazarius* in Latin, recalls to mind Nazareth and the Nazarites, and the early Christians known as Nazareans, the Nazarites among the ancient Hebrews were religious devotees who through special vows had set themselves apart (see Numbers VI) for the word *Nazar* meant 'to keep', 'guard', 'protect'.

Was the hidden meaning that these local Christians still guarded their ancient Druidic 'cromlech', now a very sacred Christian open air church? The small Christian church in Ireland was first called a Cill, and in the Isle of Man where there had been many Druids, a Keeill, the same as in Scotland where it later became a Kirk (a circle). So Celse seems to have the same radic, (it being a Celtic word) for he was a Gaul.

101

The Gallic God of Our Valley

We have already noticed that Béziers, a coastal town not far from Rennes les Bains, has a cathedral dedicated to SS Nazaire and Celse, and was probably built on the site of an early church of that name. There is a festive carnival image in Béziers of a 'camel' (as other towns have 'dragons'), which is paraded on every suitable occasion in procession around the streets. This is curious. Why do they have an oriental beast? The answer to this problem, is a little more obscure for the French who call it a *Chameau*, which comes from the Greek *Kamelos* via the Latin *Camelus* meaning 'camel', its origin however, is in the Semitic name *Gemel* for a camel, after which the third letter in the Phoenician and Jewish alphabet 'G' is called. Here we have the reminder of the importance accorded by the Druids to the number 'Three' and the Triad, also, one now clearly sees that this carnival camel is a disguised symbol reminding us of the Gallic god of war Camul, who the Romans turned into Camulus, and equated with Mars. *Camul* meant 'heaven' (literally a vaulted roof) and is equated with the Celtic God Nuada who owned an invincible sword, one of the treasures of the Tuatha Dé Danaan, also one of the most important gods of the Gaels and Britons. Similarly, Hercules was given a sword by Hermes, as he was the champion of the gods associated with hot springs like those which exist in Rennes les Bains.

Thus we have it! Camul is the original Patron god of Béziers, held in memory by the dedication of their cathedral to St Nazaire and St Celse, the latter as explained above, meaning 'high or lofty' like Camul a 'vaulted roof'.

The church at Rennes les Bains is dedicated to the same saints, and Camulus as the god of our valley is born out by the prominent connection of Mars with Montferrand. Also, with regard to the dedication of this pair of inseparable saints, it is the Age of Pisces when the Twins mark the highest point reached by the sun at the summer solstice, the Christian Era, and so we have these 'twinned' saints, joined to the same feast day, as they lived and died together. Camul or Nuada and Hercules are the Hero god and man, who climbed to the highest heaven.

Grail Connection

The four treasures of the Tuatha Dé Danaan were:

1   Sword of Nuada.
2   Lance of Lugh.
3   Cauldron of Dagda.
4   Stone of Fail (destiny).

In the Arthurian myth of the Celestial Arthur (to which the British War Leader Arthur who fought the Saxon invaders gave rise), are the Grail Legends of the Knights of the Round Table. King Arthur with his sword Excalibur, replaces Nuada and his sword, similarly Lancelot replaces Lugh and his lance, and the Holy Grail of the Last Supper is the Christian equivalent of the Cauldron of Dagda.

In our valley we have the natural 'Cromlech', the Temple (which is a Celtic word) of Camul or King Arthur (note that Arthur's castle was at Camelot), who lived around the time of the

Above: Château D'Arques. (Postcard c. 1890.) Centre: Castle ruin and village at Coustaussa. (Postcard c. 1910.) Below: Château of Couiza. (Postcard posted 1905.)

103

laying out of our Cross. According to one account he was killed in 542 AD, and another says that he was crowned in 543 at Caerleon on Usk, which is the left base angle of the triangle of the Archbishoprics corresponding to Rennes les Bains and The Devil's Chair and the Prophets. His memorial is held on the 30th of May which our alignment to La Ferrière Source commemorates, as in the case of Montferrand the word *Ferrière* refers to 'iron', whose lord is Mars, god of war, appropriate to King Arthur as it was to the centurion St Marcellus.

King Arthur's wife Gwynhwyvar ('white apparition') can be associated with the River Blanque, both named after the White Goddess or the Moon Goddess.

In the northern arm of our Cross we have the château of Serres, and in the Arthurian Legends the temple of the Holy Grail was situated in Sarras. In the earlier story of St Joseph coming to Glastonbury recorded in the *Book of Melkin*, he first landed with his companions in North Wales and was imprisoned by the wicked king. He states that "After his release by the king of Sarras, he and Joseph and ten others passed through Britain where Arviragus was reigning in the 63rd year of the Incarnation of the Lord. The king, though he rejected their message, gave them the island of *Yniswitrin* that is Glassy Isle [Glastonbury]".

Sarras or *Serres* which means a 'gorge' or 'defile', clearly comes from the Sanskrit *Saras*, a 'river'. The village and Visigothic fort of Serres that guarded the entrance of our Valley has surely taken its name from it, for it is indeed a narrow defile with high steep hills on either side. This is the entrance Sarras into the Holy Valley of the Cross, once an important Druidic Ceal ('Cromleck') christianised into the open air church of the New Jerusalem and a Temple of the Holy Grail.

In Ireland the old pagan tradition had been preserved till the last century in which the peasants always approached a sacred place from the North side, and then moved from East to West like the sun, here then the pilgrims to our Druidic Temple would have come along the River Sals from Couiza, moved south through the entrance of our Valley, visited the springs and 'Cromleck', attaching pieces of cloth from their clothes to certain bushes, offering libations to sacred stones etc.

They would then have gone West by the paths of the Maurine or Jaffus to the Holy Hill of Rennes le Château as it was later known, and returned North to Couiza having made a complete deasul circle, they may also have made a longer detour via le Bézu. The chief of the Arthurian cycle was Myrddin (Merlin in Norman French), the first name of Britain as we learn from a Triad, was 'Myrddin's Enclosure', his wife Elen was the only daughter of Coel (the British name of Camul, the Gallic god of war). Now the mother of Constantine was Helen daughter of King Cole of Colchester. No wonder that Galla Placidia was fascinated by her visit to the christianised valley of Rennes les Bains and what they told her about it.

The ancient pagans did not worship the Sky god in isolation, rather in conjunction with the Earth Mother, the marriage of whom in Spring produced the fertility of the crops and animals, for it stood for the fertilisation of the earth by the heat of the Sun and the moisture of the rains from heaven.

We have found the name of the sky god Camul; and ascertained from the River Blanque and Albedunum (le Bézu) and Blanchefort that we have here the White Goddess, the Moon Goddess.

What however, was the specific name of the Great Mother as the Earth Goddess here? The Mother Goddess of the Tuatha Dé Danaan, Danu is thought to be the same as the British goddess Anu for her name comes from *Ana* meaning 'plenty', and in Ireland at Kerry two hills are called 'the paps of Anu'. She was thus a goddess of plenty and probably a very early

Earth Mother, from whom the name of Black Annis is most likely derived, the latter was a savage woman who devoured human victims, a typical characteristic of earth goddesses.

Professor Rhys recognised the name Anu in the dative case of an inscription in Vaucluse dedicated to *Anoniredi*, 'chariot of Anu' which is confirmed by the fact that images of the fertility goddesses used to be drawn in carts through the fields by cows. Is this then the true origin of the name of Rhedae as the chariot of Anu? Has the name Anu been dropped in Christian times, thus shortened from Anoniredi to Redi or Reda, or later Rhedae. This is far more likely than the idea that it was named after the wagons of the Visigoths, because nearly all the different tribes of nomadic Celts used them, furthermore, we find the name of the Goddess Anu christianised into Anna or Anne at Arques.

The Cross of the Druids

At the beginning of the Piscean age, before our local druids had been converted to Christianity most probably by missionaries of the early British Church, who as we have seen were themselves most likely to have been converted druids, the cross of the equinoxes and solstices might have been marked out in our Valley. However, it would have been slightly different than the present alignment.

In *The Round Towers of Ireland* p.289, O'Brian quotes from Schedius (De Morib; German XXIV) the following: 'The Druids seek studiously for an Oak tree large and handsome, growing up with Two Principal arms in the form of a Cross, beside the main stem upright. If the two horizontal arms are not sufficiently adapted to the figure, they fasten a cross-beam to it. This tree they consecrate in this manner. Upon the right branch they cut in the bark, in fair characters, the word HESUS; upon the middle upright stem, the word TARAMIS; upon the left branch BELENUS; over this, above the going off of the arms, they cut the name of God THAU, under all, the same repeated THAU' (or Teutathes 'Father of the people' from whom the Gauls descended).

Thus in our Cross in the Valley, looking North as the Celts and Gauls did in their religious ceremonies, we have the alignment to the beginning of Sagittarius, which is ruled by Jupiter. In the oak tree cross, as seen above, the Druids cut the name of Taramis (meaning the 'thunderer') which the Romans rightly equated with Jupiter, in our Cross this is marked by the Devil's Chair. The chair is the throne of royalty, Osiris' name was written in hieroglyphics with an eye and a chair, the king of course was in early times the high priest of God on earth. Though the present Devil's Chair may be of dubious antiquity, the site may previously have been marked by a boulder as it was common for a rock with a prominent view to be called the Druid's seat, or King Arthur's chair.

Jupiter was associated with a rock or Baetyl, and the explanation for this was that his father Saturn, in order to save himself when old from being dethroned by one of his sons, tried to swallow all his children alive, however he was given a stone instead of the baby Jupiter, which forced him to regurgitate them all. Of course this is a crude story to explain the substitution of the worship of anthropomorphic gods for *baetyli*.

On the left side of the oak tree cross was carved 'Belenus', which corresponds to the western arm of our Cross at the Homme Mort. Belenus, Baal or Aballa as it is variously spelt, is the sun god, here in the place of the sign Pisces and of the vernal equinoctial constellation of our age, and in the West where the sun dies daily, and the Dead Man (Homme Mort) can be taken to represent the sacrifice to the Earth Goddess in the spring, and the Crucifixion of Jesus. The nearby village of Valdieu is thought to be derived from Baal dieu, the god Baal, whose alignment falls within the end of Pisces in our arrangement.

On the right arm of the Cross was cut the name of Hesus, who was the god of war, identified with Mars, to whom victims were sacrificed by being suspended upon trees and ritually wounded. We have seen how Montferrand to the north-east of our Cross was connected with Mars, and therefore in pagan times with Hesus. Hesus, Eas, or Es, was easily assimilated with Jesus, Jesu, or the Hebrew original Yesu. Instead of expecting human sacrifices bound to trees and ritually wounded, did not He Yesu, offer up himself as a sacrifice for mankind, and was He not speared with a Lance? Doubtless this was the argument of persuasion used by the early Celtic Christians with the druids and their followers, also there was the precedent of the Northern God Odin hanging on a tree for nine days in order to benefit mankind.

Camulus was equated by the Romans with Mars, so in our valley he is the same as Hesus, thus it is very fitting that this holy valley should be rededicated by the Cross to Jesus. Camulus seems to have been very popular in this region because when the young Roman coloniser Licinus Crassus founded the new town at the old Celtic Narbo (Narbonne) in 67 BC, he added the name of Mars and called it Narbo Martius. This eastern arm of our Cross represents in the calendar the sign and constellation of Virgo, which in the Piscean age is that of the autumn equinox. In the year this is the time when the sun is crucified and descends below the celestial equator, when it loses its strength and the nights grow longer and the days colder, which is probably why Hesus is here on this side of our Cross. So this may explain why the valley sacred to Camul, or Hesu, was easily converted to Jesu, and was called the Valley of the Cross.

Bier of Lazarus

I do not kow whether the Celtic Church was aware of the tradition held by the Arabic Christians of calling the Great Bear NA' ASH LAAZAR or Bier of Lazarus, whose three tail stars represented Mary, Martha and Mary Magdalen. Could Nazaire or Nazarius have suggested the above in a corrupted and shortened form as Nazar? We have seen how the feast of St Lazarus, 17th December, falls on the alignment from our Cross to the church at Cassaignes which is approximately in the north-north-west of it, this is like the Great Bear being a little to the side of the pole star.

In the 8th century the Great Bear was called the Barque of St Peter, was it previously known as the Barque of St Joseph of Arimathea, the Virgin Mary, Martha, Mary Magdalen, Lazarus and the others, in which they came to Marseilles now transferred symbolically into the sky? In Cornwall it was similary called 'King Arthurs Wain', the waggon of Rhedae again!

It is interesting to note that Polaris in the tail of the Little Bear had a declination of 81·01° in 500 AD which increased to 82·01° in 700 AD, thus decreasing its distance from the true Celestial Pole from nine to eight degrees. This covers most of the period that the Visigoths ruled over our area, and is about the same as the variation of our Cross, 8° to 8$^1/2$° from the North.

Astronomical Alignments

There are a few other interesting alignments around our Cross concerning astronomy and the calendar which we should notice. Sometimes in terrestrial alignments the difference between the highest and lowest position of the sun on the meridian, that of midday on the solstices, is recorded. This is of course caused by the axis of the earth being at an angle of $23^1/2°$ with that of the ecliptic, and as we have already stated the equator is in line, or in the same plane as the ecliptic at the equinoxes, and has a $23^1/2°$ difference North or South of it at the solstices.

In our Cross this alignment is placed 47° West of the meridian, due South. That is the same as 43° around our Cross measuring from the western arm, to which we have to add 8° — $8^1/2°$ the difference between our Cross and the true cardinal points, which gives $51^1/2°$, or the site of the Bézu Church.

Mr Guy-René Doumayrou points out in *L'Esprit des Lieux* p.111-113 that at the latitude 43° when the sun rises at 65° from the North point of the horizon (Azimuth 65°), it crosses the meridian and happens to be 65° above the horizon, then proceeds to set at 65° West of the North point (Azimuth 295°). This is of course taking the horizon to be level ground. Notice the Triad again!

This happens approximately at the time of Beltain, or more accurately on the 11th of May, and also at the time of Lugnasad, 1st of August. He calls this path of the sun the axis of Rogations 'the place of that redemption, the particular path of the metamorphosis of the Dragon'.

The Christian Rogation (Latin *rogare* to 'beseech') days were originally the Monday, Tuesday and Wednesday preceeding Holy Thursday or Ascension Day, when the Messiah ascended into Heaven forty days after His Resurrection. According to some accounts, this has been held since the year 68 AD and was extended to Ascension Week by Claude Mamert the bishop of Vienne in the south of France in the 5th century, who attached to it an annual procession with litanies, and supplications for the blessing of the fruits of the earth at this season of blossoming forth. (Note the similarity of his name with Mamers an Oscan rustic name for the god Mars.) The latitude of Vienne is $45^1/2°$, so that the above phenomena for the latitude 43° is roughly applicable.

In the countryside the processions of Rogation week often took the form of carrying the cross around the parish boundary, and it is thought that bishop Mamert incorporated into Christianity a pagan ceremony similar to the Roman Terminalia, when Jupiter, known as Terminus, god of the boundaries, was offered sacrifices. The Druidic Year was connected with the Terms, which word is derived from the god Terminus, obviously a translation of his Celtic equivalent. Terminus is thought to come from the same root as the Greek god Hermes who in his earliest form was also a boundary god. In early Greek *Hermes* meant literally 'the god of the heap of stones', thus the spirit of landmarks, so Terminus is a specialised form of Mercury, even though identified with the king of the gods Jupiter, and both Mercury and Hermes from boundary spirits developed into guardians of the roads, the protectors of travellers, and because they guarded the caravans they became also associated with commerce.

107

Bishop Mamert

It is interesting to see that his saint's day falls on the 11th of May, agreeing with the above path of the sun. Doubtless the pre-christian festival was a part of the extended Beltain or May celebrations, when the 'dragon' or the life force in nature had risen and caused the vegetation to flower, and the trees to blossom; there were however, other dragons of the elements which caused storms, fires and earthquakes that destroyed the land. This date, May 11th is in the sign of Taurus the Bull, and when the vernal equinox actually fell in the constellation of Aries, it was marked by the constellation of the Bull.

The 'horns' of the Bull, which is the night house of venus, symbolize the new moon in this fertile month of growth, and therefore in this sign the moon is Exalted, Taurus is naturally an earth sign, the beast of great strength who as an ox is so intimately connected with the agricultural toil of the earth.

This angle of the axis of Rogations being 65° East or West of North is the same as 25° North of the East or West, and as Mr Doumayrou has shown us in his book, is often marked in alignments. On our Cross, 25° North of East is $180° + 8° — 8^1/2° + 25° = 213° - 213^1/2°$, which falls nearly on the peak of Mount Cornes (Latin *Cornu* meaning 'Horn'). Thus the path of the sun of the pre-christian 'fixed' path of ascension is marked by the 'horns' of the new moon and those of the Bull or Taurus. The devil who is always portrayed with horns, 'Old Horny', probably originated from the memory of the pagan god Cernunnos, the antlered god of Gaul, who had a torque hanging from each of them, and was probably the Lord of Beasts, apparently remembered here in the appellation of Mount Cornes.

If we take the path of the sun when it is 65° East or West of the southern meridian, we also have approximately the time of Oimelc (Candlemas), and Samhain.

Then we look for an alignment in the West, $0° + 8° — 8^1/2° + 25° = 33° — 33^1/2°$. This falls 1° short of the ruin situated on the Serre Mijane ($34^1/2°$) giving us the 25th of March in the calendar, the Annunciation of the Virgin Mary, which dates from the 6th century. Similarly in the East we have $180° + 8° — 8^1/2° - 25° = 163° — 163^1/2°$, which is that of the source near les Carbounières on the way to Sougraigne and represents the 6th of August and the Transfiguration of Christ, a festival instituted by the Greek Church as early as 700 AD, but not by the Latin until 1456 AD. Nevertheless, this festival was observed in Spain earlier in the time of St Ildefonse, Bishop and Patron of Toledo, who mentions it. (He died in 669 AD.) Since Toledo was the capital of the Visigoths after the fall of Toulouse, it is quite possible that it was known locally when our Cross was constructed.

Pentagrams and the Druidic Year

In our first two pentagrams of the vertical masculine axis of the Cross we have all the months of the year except January and July, similarly, in the third and fourth pentagrams of the feminine horizontal arms of the Cross are all the months except April and October. These four months halve and quarter the year. January and July are the months which determine the two halves of our our Druidic Year, and the Calendar which used to inform us of the daily agricultural activity. Thus these four months roughly associate the agricultural year with the beginning of the four seasons. November and May are at the apex of the first and second pentagrams and were surely connected with the heliacal rising of the Pleiades, their constellation Taurus, and its opposite Scorpio.

These months divide the year approximately into the winter and summer halves when either darkness and cold, or light and heat predominate. We recall the 'death of Osiris' on the 17th of Hathor (26th November) and Herodotus informs us that there was a festival of the 'finding of Osiris' on the 19th of Pakhons (23rd May) which is that of his resurrection in spring. Similarly, the 22nd of November is at the apex of our first Pentagram and 21st of May at that of the second.

We have seen how St Saturnin was dragged by a bull to his death at Toulouse and how this was associated with the celestial phenomenon, his festival is held on the 29th of November and falls on the octave of the sun entering the sign Sagittarius. This is similar to the 'death of Osiris' and of the vegetation of summer, and is also near the apex of our first Pentagram, and the saint is marked by the Church of Peyrolles whose dedication is the same as that to which it aligns in our calendar. It seems certain that the Visigoths knew about the Druidic Year, and also these pentagrams, for which they deliberately aligned the markers.

The first Pentagram of Diana the moon goddess orientates the Cross to the North,which represents the signs of the lower hemisphere and the winter half of the year. The second Pentagram of Apollo the sun god points to the South, that of the upper hemisphere and summer half. In the former, after the autumn equinox, the nights grow longer and the days shorter, the weather also becomes colder causing the vegetation to die down and then the leaves begin to fall, which becomes very apparent in November. In the latter the converse is the case, following the vernal equinox everything springs forth into life, and thrives in May, these two halves of the year have been taken from time immemorial to represent the annual fight of life and light against death and darkness. These two pentagrams therefore correctly belong to the vertical axis of spirit, and its fight against death and darkness, or the death and resurrection of the god of life and vegetation in the year. Because of this we have the apex of each pentagram placed on the head of the Microcosmic Man, inverted and falling in the first Pentagram, and erect and rising in the second.

Similarly, the Microcosmic Woman of the horizontal arms of our Cross of matter has her head in the apex of the third Pentagram of the god Pan and Fertility which falls in the middle of February, following the festival of the purification of the earth at Candlemas where she represents the Great Creative Mother Goddess. In the fourth Pentagram the Microcosmic Woman's head falls on the 23rd of August when the sun enters the sign of Virgo, the time of the harvest and here shows the aspect of the Great Mother in her destructive aspect of autumn.

Halves of the Druidic Year recorded around the Cross

As we know the Druidic Year begins in January and its second half in July, both of these months are conspicuous by being omitted in the first and second pentagrams. In the third, the marker for the point on which we have July aligns with Bugarach Church, and the day is that of St Hermagoras on the 12th, falling in the sign of Cancer and the moon. The fourth Pentagram holds the month of January whose marker is the Aram ruin, and the day the 11th of St Hyginus and also St Theodosius, which is in the sign of Capricorn of the agricultural deity Saturn (in both cases on the Microcosmic Woman's right foot).

Now Bugarach church (139°) is almost opposite the Aram ruin (321° — exactly opposite would be 319°) on one side and those of Jaffus (316$\frac{1}{2}$°) on the other.

321° Aram ruin

Aram or Aramea is the biblical name for what is now called Syria and beyond, it was thought to come from the Hebrew word *Aram* meaning 'to be high' or 'to exalt oneself', which may have been the origin of the Greek word *Hermes; Aram* meant the 'Highlands', not inappropriate for this area. The highest point of this Pentagram falls in Virgo whose ruler is Mercury or Hermes. The day of the alignment to the Aram ruin is the 11th of Januray whose saints are Hyginus and Theodosius, (from Hygeia the Greek goddess of health personified, and 'the gift of God').

316¹/₂° Jaffus ruins, 6th January. Epiphany (probably instituted in 813 AD)

The Domain of Jaffus which was once the site of an ancient church and little monastery, was destroyed by fire in 1891, thus very suitably aligned with such an important festival as The Three Kings.

Bugarach Church

This is situated under the highest mountain in the region from which it take its name. It marks the 12th of July in the calendar and the festival of St Hermagoras, bishop of Aquila and disciple of St Mark, whose name is derived from Hermes.

It is most interesting to find St Mark's disciple here, for as well as founding the Coptic Church, St Mark is traditionally supposed to have sent St Aristobulos the father-in-law of St Peter to be the first bishop of Britain, which could be considered as evidence of the local Celtic Church with its British connection being present at the laying out of our Cross. Hence Bugarach Church and the Aram and Jaffus ruins mark the months of the two halves of the Druidic Year, a fact which was apparently known at that time, and was it not at Bugarach village an ancient pageant took place on Ash Wednesday with the Hermit carrying the cross with the horse-collar hung with bells and sausages, preserving for us the clue leading to St Anthony the Hermit, the Hermitage and the end of the Druidic Year?

A Druidic Year Marker

330¹/₂° Roc d'en Clots and ruins at Borde du Loup
Sun enters Aquarius   20th January. Juno, goddess. St Fabian, pope, martyr. 236 AD.
*   St Sebastian, martyr. 287 AD.*
*   21st January St Agnes, martyr. 305 AD.*

These two places mark the third and fourth intercalary days of our Druidic Year, if we extend this alignment it falls appropriately on the place called the Pas du Loup.

In Northern mythology the Fenris Wolf was the son of Loki, both of whom were to be released at the end of the Age (Ragnarok), they would then fight their enemies the gods, and in the conflict mutually destroy one another, thus bringing about the end of the world. The intercalary days were an addition to the ancient Egyptian year, discovered at a later date, in order to measure it more accurately, and were therefore considered to be outside the year. This was the time of the birth of the five, gods and goddesses, of the Osirian cycle and so would also be the end of an age.

110

We have have here the Wolf (Loup), and it may be that St Lupus has been substituted for the Celtic sun god Lug, and this alignment marks the time that the sun enters the sign of Aquarius and three days later the Druidic Year begins.

Wolves were one of the greatest enemies of early man, attacking him and his herds, and it is interesting to recall that the Saxons called this month of January the Wolf Month. This was because the extreme cold and snow meant that wolves could not find sufficient prey, therefore it was the time that men and their flocks were in greatest danger.

The Moon's Eclipse Cycle

There is another interesting angle hidden around our Cross which is connected with the moon. The moon's path is inclined about 5° to the ecliptic, the sun's maximum declination is $\pm 23^1/2°$, so therefore the moon's maximum declination is $\pm 28^1/2°$ and its minimum $\pm 18^1/2°$. These are called the Major and Minor Standstills and it takes the moon about 9·3 years to move from one to the other, therefore the whole cycle is 18·61 years, in which the eclipses occur at the same calendar dates.

The Megalithic people and later observers could have noticed the Major Standstill by observing the point on the horizon of the moon rise and set, and could thus have known the eclipse season. In our Cross the Major Standstill of the moon for $+ 28^1/2°$ is recorded thus:

	Western arm of the Cross	360°
Plus	Moon's Maximum declination	- $28^1/2°$
	Cross deviation from true north	+ 8° — $8^1/2°$
	which gives us	$339^1/2°$ — 340°

This then is marked by the alignment to Rennes le Château Church (340°). We may have to add half a degree to the above as they may not have taken into account Refraction which causes it to be seen before it really has reached the horizon. This is then only 1° or $1^1/2°$ short of our marker the Maurine Spring ($341^1/2°$) of the first arm of our first and lunar Pentagram of Brighid and Candlemas. It is very appropriate to see the moon and its cycle associated with Candlemas, the time of the purification of the earth, and that of the Great Mother, when the seeds which lay dormant in the ground in winter then germinate and spring to life.

We also have a ruin at $37^1/2°$ which similarly would mark the Major Standstill as -$28^1/2°$. Thus $28^1/2°$ plus $^1/2°$ for refraction and 8° to $8^1/2°$ adjustment for our Cross, gives us 37° to $37^1/2°$, which is to be found at the bottom of Pas de la Roque. It aligns with the 28th of March, the day of St Gontran, king and grandson of Clovis I, founder of the Merovingian dynasty and his Queen St Clotilde. Gontran lived from 525 until 593 AD. This marker has therefore been 'arranged' by the Merovingians at a later date.

$45^1/2°$ les Gavignauds ruins. 6th April.
St Marcellinus, martyr, 413 AD.

This alignment, which has not found a place on our figures, falls in the middle of the sign Aries in our calendar around the Cross, which is the Day House of mars, its saint's name

Marcellinus is similar to that of St Marcellus of the alignment to the Château Montferrand both being derived from the God Mars, and the latter falls in Scorpio being the Night House of the planet mars.

Here is hidden an interesting measure, for from les Gavingnauds ruins at $45^1/2°$ to that of Montferrand Château at $247°$ is $201^1/2°$, similarly back around the other side of the circle is $158^1/2°$ ($201^1/2° + 158^1/2° = 360°$).

Now around the time of the setting out of our Cross, in 500 AD the third star in the belt of Orion called Alnitak had a Right Ascension (celestial longitude) $66·45°$, similarly the Royal Star Antares in Scorpio was $225·09°$, the difference between them being $158·64°$. Thus we see that the shortest distance between these two markers is from Château Montferrand to the ruins of les Gavignauds $158^1/2°$ which is the same as these two stars in 500 AD.

This seems to refer to the myth of Orion the hunter who was killed by a scorpion and immortalized in the constellations. Scorpio is opposite Taurus and its paranatellon Orion, so that when the former rises the latter set and vice-versa. In the year, when the sun enters Scorpio in autumn, the fertile bull (Taurus) of the summer half and Orion 'die', and so does the vegetation. Plutarch informs us that Osiris was murdered by Set 'when the sun was in Scorpio on the 17th day of Hathor', that is to say when the Full Moon (here identified with Osiris) began to wane in November. Sahu (Orion) was the resting place of the soul of Osiris until he was re-born in May, and this story refers to the 'Death' and 'Finding' of Osiris, or the sowing and reaping of wheat in lower Egypt, etcetera.

In the case of St Saturnin the myth has been modified for Christian usage. As he was killed by a bull he can neither be figured by Orion or Taurus which set or 'die' together, nor by Scorpio which was considered to be the symbol of 'death' and the Fall.

I think that St Saturnin was represented by Ophiuchus a paranatellon of Scorpio. At the time of the autumn equinox when the sun was in Libra, just after sunset, the Bull would be seen rising on the eastern horizon and the Scorpion with Ophiuchus setting or 'dying' in the West. They are then figuratively 'joined' by the 'rope' of the horizon, as was St Saturnin to the bull which dragged him to his death. When the sun has entered Scorpio it disappears with Ophiuchus from the night sky and after sunset a triumphant Taurus is seen rising in the East.

Ophiuchus was identified with Æsculapius the god of medicine, by the Greeks and Latins, and as we have noted (p.69) was acceptable to the early Christians. As a constellation he is depicted struggling which with a snake (evil), above which is that of a Crown; so he is very suitable to represent St Saturnin, who overcoming the fear of death for Christ received the martyr's crown.

St Saturnin died in 250 AD, and the Coptic calendar dates from 284 AD, which shows that from the 17th to the 20th of Hatur (the four days of mourning for Osiris in ancient Egypt) correspond to our 26th to 29th of November. It also gives the 19th of Hatur as the day to 'Avoid voyaging in the Mediterranean Sea'.

Around 500 AD when our Cross had just been laid out, Alnitak culminated at midnight on the 28th of November marking the end of the sailing season and Ophiuchus culminated at midday on the 29th symbolizing the ascension of St Saturnin into Heaven. Doubtless the merchants of Toulouse observed this date from pre-christian times, and there Christianity seems to have replaced an Isis cult.

It is also appropriate to find here St Marcellinus because Salazar in his Spanish martyrology asserts that he was a native of Toledo which became the Visigothic capital after the fall of Toulouse.

The Great Mother

Our Cross is not oriented to true North but to the Château of Serres which in our calendar indicates the 22nd of November sacred to the goddess Diana, one of whose forms was the goddess of the Ephesians, wearing a castellated crown and having many breasts, whose cult was widely spread and seems appropriate here.

Nearby, at Arques the fairs were held on the 26th of July and the 18th of October. That of the 26th of July commemorates the falling asleep of St Anne, mother of the Virgin Mary and grandmother of Jesus, whose festival was very popular in Brittany, she also is Patron of the church at Arques. Clearly St Anne has supplanted the worship of the Celtic Great Mother Goddess Danu, Anu, or Ana as she was variously called.

The château of Arques marks in the calendar around our Cross the 21st of October of St Hilarion and also St Ursula and her 11,000 Virgins, martyred in 453 AD. In the Alternative Arrangement clockwise around the Cross, it marks the day of St Anna, the prophetess who foretold the future greatness of the infant Jesus in the Temple, again the Celtic Ana.

The fair of the 18th of October is that of St Luke the evangelist who alone relates to us the story of the conception and birth of Christ, his symbol was in the constellation Taurus, the Bull, the zodiacal sign for Spring.

Horn Fair

Though we do not know anything about this ancient October fair of Arques, nonetheless we can ascertain its main features from the fair in London at the village of Charlton which was also held on St Luke's day. This festival was particularly connected with horns, they were worn by the holiday-makers, and adorned every booth, Ram's horns were on sale in abundance, and even the gingerbread was marked by a pair of gilt horns. These horns were the signature of St Luke's Bull, and the crescent moon. Unusual license was practised and it was customary for the men to wear woman's clothes, they chased the women and beat them with furze, for as they used to say "all was fair at Horn Fair". This whipping of women was often practised in ancient festivals like that of the Lupercalia of the God Pan and Mother Goddess Juno, to produce fecundity.

The dressing up of the men in woman's vestments points to the festival of the Great Mother Goddess to whom were ascribed the fertility of the earth and its creatures and their fruitfulness.

At Arques, pigs were brought to this fair, and pigs, especially the wild boars, were sacred animals to the Celts for they ate the acorns that fell on the ground from the oak trees held to be holy by the Druids. The fairs probably lasted for several days around the beginning of the Christian period, for even the more important fairs of the last century lasted for two or three weeks. Thus we have here on its eve the 17th of October which, as we have seen corresponds to the 17th of the month when the Ark of Noah grounded at Ararat, then the mountain, a 'breast' of the Earth, arose from the fresh waters, or was 'born'.

This date was marked by the alignment to Arques Church, and was also suggested by the mountain peak above called La Berco Grando, which we have associated with Noah's Ark, the Ark is in a sense a symbol of the womb of the Great Mother from which figuratively all creatures are born and nourished. Thus the image of Artemis has many breasts and various animals including the bulls displayed on her dress. We have here over the festive period of the fair:

- 17th October the Eve, marked by Arques Church. The grounding of the Ark.
- 18th October St Luke's day, the Fair of Horns.
- 21st October St Hilarion.

St Ursula and her 11,000 Virgins

The legend informs us that Ursula was a British girl who was on her way to join her future husband Conan Meriadec in Brittany, but because of a gale her boat was driven off course and they travelled up the Rhine to be cut off. She and all her entourage were massacred by the Huns at Cologne. Her name is thought to be the same as the Swabian Goddess Hörsel or Ursel, the equivalent of the Teutonic Holda (Venus), I think that this suggests the Little Bear (Ursa Minor) with the countless stars or 11,000 Virgins circling around the Pole Star in its tail as Ursula.

Peyrolles

Nearby to Arques is the village of Peyrolles whose church is both dedicated to and correctly aligns with St Saturnin (29th of November), who was killed by a bull at Toulouse, and who, as we have seen 'dies' with the constellation of the Archer at this time in the West at sunset, whilst that of the Bull rises triumphant in the eastern sky.

The god Saturn, from whom his name is derived, is connected with the element Earth and therefore he is the divine husbandman who ploughs the earth with the Ox, sows the seed and harvests the crops. This god is closest to Mother Earth.

We have seen how Peyrolles village probably received its name from the stream which in turn appears to be named after the menhir called the Peyro Dreto. This stands about half way between Peyrolles and Arques, and was very probably the site of the funeral ground of the latter pagan and early Christian times, for it was the custom to bury the dead at some distance from the human habitations. Thus the barrow and later burial ground, which amongst the Celts were circular and situated within an enclosure, were from the pagan usage converted for the Christians by the presence of the anchorite's cell, oratory and cross, and the fair was always held nearby. I strongly suspect that the fairs of Arques were therefore sited near this menhir, and this stone appropriately aligns with All Souls day in our calendar, which we have already discussed.

Everything that we have found out about this region strongly indicates the special worship of the Great Mother Goddess Anu or Ana which has come down to us through the cult of St Anne whose fête is the 26th of July.

We also have St Mary Magdalen, 22nd July (marked by the Alternative Arrangement clockwise around the Cross by the church of Peyrolles), who has clearly taken the place of an erotic Gallic deity similar to the Roman Venus of sex and fertility. She probably marked the beginning, and Ana the end of the summer fair at Arques, as it occurred at the moment of Harvest and the gifts of the earth. Six days after the festival of St Anne or within its octave, is Lugnasad, the Christian Lammas or rather Lambmass called thus because St Peter as the shepherd of Christ's Church was expected to follow Jesus' injunction 'to feed my sheep'. Also, it was the day of St Peter in chains which is marked by Serres Church. On Lugnasad were commemorated the Nuptials of the Sky Father and the Earth Mother.

Black and White Virgins

In 813 AD, the sepulchre of St James the Great was 'discovered' at Compostella and he was claimed to be the apostle and patron of Spain, his day is on the eve of that of St Anne, on the 25th of July, that of St Magdalen on the 22nd of July begins the half of the year that ends with St Anthony's fête the 17th of January. This is the dark, feminine or lunar half of the Druidic Year, approximately corresponding to the dark half of the moon and St John the Baptist's half in the current 365 day year.

If one adds 180 days, or half a Coptic year to the festivals of St James and St Anne then this ends with the 20th and 21st of January, the former being in the middle, and both fall in the Intercalary Days. We thus have:

- July 22nd St Mary Magdalen to 17th January St Anthony.
- July 25th St James, apostle and Patron of Spain, to 20th January and St Fabian and St Sebastian of Narbonne, patron of the Kingdom of Oviedo in Spain. Sun enters Aquarius.
- July 26 St Anne, grandmother of Jesus to 21st January St Agnes.

The great mediaeval pilgrimage to Santiago de Compostella on the northern coast of Spain, particularly followed the route from the East of Provence along the Pyrenees and down to Compostella, which is roughly East to West like the apparent daily path of the Sun. This route also seems to divide Gaul in the North from Spain in the South, as the celestial equator divides the upper constellations of spring and summer from those lower ones of autumn and winter. The whole of this pilgrim route goes through an area particularly well endowed with megalithic monuments, and St James' particular emblem from Compostella is the Scallop Shell, an emblem that is associated with the Great Mother Goddess coming from the underworld of the deep sea. The main pilgrimage is born like the sun in the East and travels to the West to end or die at Compostella, or its annual passage from the vernal to the autumn equinoxes. The journey ends near the sea after passing all these megalithic sites and burial grounds, and seems to be very much associated with some pre-christian worship of the Great Goddess.

According to the legend, St James appeared on a horse with a great sword and encouraged the hard pressed Christians to rally and beat the Moors at the battle of Clavijo in 841 AD. Since that time it has been claimed that he also appeared and fought in battles in Flanders, Italy, India and America.

We have seen how St James' half year ends with the 20th of January, when the sun enters Aquarius ruled by the God Saturn, who as we have remarked is so closely associated with the earth. Here also is another saint claimed by Spain, St Sebastian who is the patron saint of soldiers ending that which began with St James as a knight on his horse.

The morrow, and we have already noted how adjoining saint's days are often related, is that of St Anne the Grandmother, covering the pagan Anu mother of the Celtic Gods. Her half year ends with St Agnes, the most important female saint of the early church, whose name was derived from *Agnus* a 'lamb', in the sense that it was a sacrificial lamb for a burnt offering, Agni the Sacrificial Fire and name of the Vedic Fire God, became *Ignis* (Latin for 'fire'). Jesus himself, who by his crucifixion abolished the need for all sacrifices, was Himself symbolised by the Paschal Lamb, a very popular image in the early church.

Following our analogy, the sun rises in the morning, like the holocaust in the smoke, which was always an offering to the Sky God, and sets in the evening, disappearing below the horizon, but in those sacrifices to the Earth Mother and related chthonic gods the blood was spilled into a hole in the ground. Hence the pagan burnt offering to the Sky God at the beginning of the pilgrimage in the East, and a blood one to the Earth Goddess in the West at its end, were replaced by the worship of Jesus as the Paschal lamb in the East and that of His mother Mary in the West.

The Black and the White Virgins, as Mary, always have an infant Jesus on their laps, like the birth and youth of the diurnal sun in the East, but its old age and death in the West, followed by the dark of night, are like the crucifixion with the Virgin Mary and other women who helped in washing and laying out the dead body in the tomb. This same allegory of the Day and Night, was also applied by most of the ancient religions to the Summer and Winter halves of the year, divided by the two equinoxes. With the Celts, they regarded their gods as the conquering heroes, belonging to the White Goddess, day and summer, whilst the gods of the conquered aborigines, we call the Iberian race, were those of the Black Goddess, night and winter. But though they were the rulers, nevertheless both sets of deities continued to be propitiated, because though there is less activity at night and in winter than in the day and summer, both together go to make up the whole. Soon after the 'discovery' of the sepulchre of St James at Compostella the 'invention' and worship of Black Virgins became very popular and widespread, pilgrimages took place to visit their shrines, and in a sense this is the extension of the visit to the fairs held at the barrows or graveyards of the ancestors. Thus whilst the White Goddess was replaced by the Virgin Mary of the conquering Christian religion, the Black Goddess who had been continually secretly worshipped by the country folk, was later replaced by the Virgin Mary as the Black Virgin and so could be openly worshipped.

These Black Virgins were also often found by the Ox when ploughing, and some may originally have been images of Isis with the child Horus on her knee, afterwards they were probably deliberately buried to be 'discovered' by some naive ploughman.

When the vegetation had died down in winter the Black Earth Mother guarded and germinated the seeds in her womb, which were to shoot forth as vegetation in the Spring, it was for this reason that caves, grottoes and other entrances to the underworld were held as sacred by the pagans. There, buried in the ground, also rested the hallowed ancestors, thus the Black Virgins of Christian times perpetuated the tradition in their churches and cathedrals by being placed in the underground crypts, or in grotto shrines.

The crypt of Chartres Cathedral for instance, is thought once to have been the dwelling sacred to the image of the goddess Isis who always holds her child Horus on her lap. The

Black Virgins therefore represented the dark, winter half of the year, whilst the White Virgins that of the bright summer half of the Sky Goddess.

The Black Virgin or Earth Mother bore and nourished 'life' in her womb, as did Mary for Jesus, whilst the White Virgin or Sky Goddess watched over the growth and 'life' on earth, likewise did Mary for Jesus from His infancy to His crucifixion.

The Black Virgin is prayed to for the 'release of prisoners from their chains', presumably because she as Earth Mother releases the vegetation in the Spring. Whilst the White Goddess or Virgin watches over life in the active half of the year, or the manifestation of the physical world, the Black Goddess or Virgin similarly tends the spiritual life in sleep or 'death' when the soul recuperates and the body rests.

The Celts regarded the sea, with its undrinkable salt water that also kills vegetation, as belonging to the underworld and the Black Goddess, unlike fresh water so necessary to all life which was the gift of the sky, and the domain of the White Goddess. (For the same reason in Ancient Egypt the ocean belonged to Set and the Nile to Osiris.)

Here in our valley we have the River Blanque of the White Goddess which ends or 'dies' in the river Sals (Salty one) of the Black Goddess. Around the Arques area we have seen that there are many indications pointing to the worship in pagan times of the Black Goddess, the Great Earth Mother. We have come across the bull as the sign Taurus, killing St Saturnin, or as the symbol of St Luke and his Horns Fair, and even Anu's chariot drawn by sacred cows which gave the name of Rhedae to our valley.

The sun was thought of by the ancients as the solar Ox ploughing the ecliptic as it travelled around the constellations during the year, Saturn was the god of the husbandman, who tilled the earth.

There is also at the church in Serres, marked by dedication and the alternative arrangement around the Cross, the Celtic festival of Lugnasad or the sun god Lug, the God of light, this day is that of the Christian Lammas and also that of St Peter in chains. The legend is that St Peter was imprisoned by the Jews in Jerusalem and miraculously released by an angel of the Lord, which clearly points to an attribute of the Black Virgin.

We have also come across St Anne, St Anna and St Mary Magdalen also found at Rennes le Château, which point to the pagan goddesses which they have replaced. The only thing we have not discovered is any mention of the shrine of a Black Virgin which one would have thought should have once existed here.

The Pillar and the Decans

We have found, and proved by its alignments, our Cross in the Valley as laid out by the Visigoths. We can go further into the question, did they know about the Druidic Year? Did they also associate St Anthony and St Magdalen with the vertical and horizontal arms of this Cross? In the case of the Druid's chair, nicknamed the Devil's Armchair, the Cathedra of St Peter in Rome was at that time celebrated on the 22nd of February. The change of date to the 18th of January is found in an old martyrology dating from 720 AD. However, we learn from Gregory of Tours who lived in the 6th century, that the festival of the Virgin Mary was held in Gaul in the middle of January, which the Hieran Martyrology of Gaul gives as the 18th of January. This could then have been her throne.

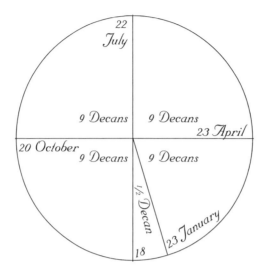

Fig. 19. Pillar and Decans.

We have seen how the year ended with the day of St Anthony the 17th of January, the day on which Theodosius was supposed to have died. In the Processional Cross carved on the Visigothic Pillar we saw that the gems seemed to give various references to the calendar:

- the 30 days of the month (especially true of the Coptic).
- 24 half lunar months
- 19 years of the Metonic cycle.
- 52 weeks of the year.
- 37 the 36 Decans and the Intercalary days.

The upper arm with 23 gems and the lower with 29 add up to the 52 weeks of the year, and form the vertical beam of the Cross, the horizontal bar has 18 gems on its left arm, and 19 on the right. We can thus put the calendar around it. (See Fig. 19.)

On the right side of the foot of the Cross are now the five Intercalary days, the 18th to the 22 of January inclusive, with the first half of the Druidic Year from the 23rd of January to the 21st of July. This is signified by the 19 gems (1 + 18), or decans.

The left side from the top of the Cross, starts the other half from the 22nd of July to the 17th of January, the 18 decans or gems. We now find that the arms of the Cross divide the year of 30 day months as follows:

    On the right side
        1 Gem Half a Decan the Intercalary days. 18th to 22nd January inclusive.
        9 Gems 9 Decans. 23rd January to the 22nd April.
        9 Gems 9 Decans. 23rd April to the 21st of July.
    On the Left side
        9 Gems 5 Decans. 22nd July to the 19th October
        9 Gems 9 Decans. 20th October to the 17th January.

Thus after the Intercalary days we have the year beginning with 'the memorial of our first parents Adam and Eve', as recorded in the English Sarum Martyrology, on the 23rd of January.

Later, after our Cross had been laid out (if in 448 AD), this day was given to St John the Almoner by the North African Church at Alexandria where he had been the Patriarch, and died at Amathus in Cyprus, his native town, on the 11th of November 619 AD, which is his memorial day in the Greek Church. He was the Patron saint of the Hospitallers, called The Knights of St John of Jerusalem.

Much later in the 16th century, when the Turkish Emperor made a gift of his remains which had rested in Constantinople to the King of Hungary, the Roman Martyrology then gave him this fête day of the 23rd of January as the 'so called day' of the translation of his relics, though really the date of his Alexandrian memorial.

The fact that he was given this especial date of the Druidic Year, its commencement, well known to the Celtic Church as we have found, demonstrates that the church at Alexandria knew all about it and goes to support the claim of the British Church to have been associated with the Coptic Church whose founder St Mark the Evangelist they said sent St Joseph of Arimathea to Britain.

St George

The next quarter of the year as marked by the right arm of the Cross starts with the 23rd of April, the day of St George. In ancient Greece this was also the day on which traditionally the animals were taken up into the hills to graze, and may have been the same in the south of Gaul.

St Magdalen's Day

The second half of the year starts with St Mary Magdalen's day, the 22nd of July, followed closely by that of St Anne on the 26th.

St Mary Salome

The last quarter as divided by the left arm of the Cross begins with the fête of St Mary Salome, mother of St James and St John on the 20th of October, and ends with that of St Anthony the Hermit on the 17th of January.

We have therefore on the right, masculine side of this Cross the solar half of the year when the sun ascends into the heaven; and conversely on the left, feminine, and lunar half the time when the moon ascends.

In the third quarter, or beginning of the second half, we have the harvest and vintage, when are gathered in the fruits of the earth. In the beginning of this is the first Arques Fair of St Anne, and on the eve of its end, the second Fair of Horns of St Luke on the 18th of October. This is very remarkable, the so called 'new date' of this fair according to Albert Fabre in his *History of Arques* 1855, is the 20th of October, day of St Mary Salome on which the last quarter begins, and which is also as one of the points of our second Pentagram of Apollo and the Christian Church.

VII Figures with Zodiacal Signs

The Triangle

We recall how the Druids had the 'arrow' of three equal arms (not joined at the point) as a religious symbol, and how in their poetry they were so fond of finding Triads of things. In Britain they had three sacred centres, and the historian Geoffrey of Monmouth (1100 - 1154) says that the Archflamens (Archdruids) of London, York and the City of Legions (Caerlion), became Archbishops in King Lucius' reign, and that the City of Legions was situated on the River Usk in Monmouthshire. (Book 4 cap: XIX.) St David later removed the site of the Archiepiscopal See from the City of Legions to his birthplace Menevia, now called St David's, where he became the Archbishop, similarly that of London was removed by St Augustine to Canterbury. If we look at the map of England we see these places make a nearly regular isoceles triangle, the angle at Caerleon is about 66°, London 73° and the apex at York 41°. In our region, the churches at Couiza, Arques and the Bézu, are dedicated to St John the Baptist, making a large Triangle with its apex at the Bézu in the South.

The Welsh druids baptised children and it appears that the Irish druids did likewise, and we can assume that the local druids did the same, this would account for the fact that the rite of Baptism, as practised by the ascetic St John was so popular in the Celtic Church, and this local Triangle of his churches. We now have within this Triangle, a nearly perfect equilateral Triangle formed by the two churches of the Rennes and that of Bézu, again at its apex. We should remember that an equilateral triangle is both a symbol of perfection in man, and also of the Holy Trinity. The apex was clearly the Jasse de Bézu, and the church just below has been erected to turn this religious site into a Christian one.

So we have the churches of St Nazaire and Celse (which also implies the presence of St Joseph of Arimathea) in the East, St Mary Magdalen in the West and St John the Baptist in the South.

In the larger Triangle of the St John's, from the church of Couiza to that of the Bézu, the site passes very near to Rennes le Château where there was once another church of St John the Baptist. Now in our equilateral Triangle we have:

- In the South the Road protected by the hill of Bézu.
- In the East the Valley and River of Rennes les Bains.
- In the West the Mountain of Rennes le Château.
- In the Middle the Wood of Lauzet

Was this latter wood the site of a druidic Nemeton?

The word *Lauzet* seems to come from the same root as the Occitan word 'Las' and *Lausat* 'praise', thus a skylark is called a Lauseta. This compares with the Latin *Laus, laudis*, 'praise', 'fame', 'glory', verb *laudo*, and the lark is called *Alauda* (a word of Gallic origin), which was also the name of a Legion formed by Julius Caesar in Gaul, probably they had crested helmets. It would seem that the lark had a special significance to the Gauls, could it have been a sacred bird that represented the druids? What could be a more suitable name for a Nemeton with the Bards and Ovates singing and chanting hymns of praise to the gods than the Wood of Praise or poetically the Wood of the Skylarks?

With regard to beautiful song and music I cannot help recalling the Ancient British belief that the music of the Druids' harps wafted the souls of the dead into heaven. These harps were triangular with three strings, and could be taken as a symbol of our equilateral Triangle.

le Bézu

This was known as Albe Dunum, comparable to the ancient name of Lyons in France and Leyden in Holland whose name was *Lug Dunum*, or the fort of Lug (the god), a typical Celtic name. So we have here the Fort of Albe, now in Latin *Albus, a, um* which means 'white', therefore the above is synonymous to the Blanque river's name, England was called *Albion*

Le Bézu Church.

supposedly from the fact that the first view of it when sailing across the Channel is its chalk cliffs, and similarly in Europe the Alps were named from their snow covered peaks.

These are all associated with the White Goddess, the Moon as the Great Mother. Even the protomartyr of Britain was called St Alban, and his day is the 22nd of June, the day following the summer solstice, when the moon is born, it is then at its lowest on the meridian, similar to the birthday of St John the Baptist, placed there for the same reason.

When the fort of Blanchefort was built in the valley of Rennes les Bains, it obviously took its name via the river from the same goddess.

Road

The fort of the Bézu guarded the old Celtic (?) and Roman road that ran here through the plain of Lauzet and continued on through the country to the Pyrenees and Spain. This plain was the scene of many battles and the fort of the Bézu was very ancient, from its Latin name we learn that it was Celtic, and it was obviously used by the Visigoths who are thought to have erected a fort here, to become a Château in the middle ages.

Pythagorean Figures, Their Meaning

The sage Pythagoras gathered a lot of the ancient wisdom and explained it geometrically. He taught that the number *one* was masculine and produced the *dual*, feminine, this is illustrated by a single point, and the dual, a line joining two points.

A *third* point, when joined to the other two points, produces the first figure a triangle. This is the father, mother and child of the ancient Trinity, the Hindus express this in Vedanta as the Seer, Seeing and Seen, which is in Grammar the subject, verb and object. Thus we have the numbers One, Two and Three.

Four, is represented by the Square or Cross, it consists of two dimensions height and width, the positive, male, vertical axis of Spirit; and the negative or rather receptive, female, horizontal axis of matter.

Five, the figure of a Pentagram, symbolising the five elements, of Earth, Water, Air, Fire and Ether the vehicle of Spirit, the five senses, etc.

Six, whose figure is the Hexagon, is made inside the Hexagram of the intertwined upright and inverted triangles called the Shield of Solomon.

Pythagorean Figures, and le Bézu and the Rennes

We have found our nearly perfect equilateral Triangle formed by the Jasse de Bézu or its Church, the Church of Rennes les Bains, and that of Rennes le Château.

Square or Cross

We have also found the Cross, looking South like the Triangle whose apex is the Bézu. The vertical axis is marked by the Hermitage by the river in the South, and the Devil's Chair on the hillside in the North, the horizontal axis is indicated by the Source of the Madeleine in the East and the pasturage of the Homme Mort in the West.

122

Pentagram (First)

This we found looking South in the Cross itself, whose inverted point or angle links it to the northern arm of the Cross, marked by the Druid's or Devil's Chair (270°). But this Pentagram has another special feature, it is linked to the apex of the large Triangle itself because its angle at 54° points straight to the nearest marker, Bézu Church at $51^1/2°$ of Ezekiel. He was the prophet who had the vision of the new Jerusalem with its new temple, brought down to earth here as our sacred Triangle of the Druids.

It is also joined to the western angle of the Triangle, for Rennes le Château is at 340° and marker of this point is the Maurine Spring at $341^1/2°$ linking it with St Bridget and Candlemas, the other pentagrams are not linked in the same way to the Triangle. This then is the first Pentagram, for it connects the Earth to the Equilateral Triangle of the Sky and Heaven, in the same manner as the Body is united with the Spirit. It is therefore that of the Great Mother manifesting herself through Nature, and the Triangle belongs to the Sky Father. The fifth Pentagram represents her formless state as Ether, the womb of the other elements.

The northern point of this Pentagram aligns with the Cross to the 22nd of November, festival of the Goddess Diana, showing that the Romans were attracted to the hot springs of Rennes les Bains and the hunting of wild boar sacred to Diana. They certainly had shrines here, maybe to Æsculapius and Diana, as has been indicated by local discoveries. What is interesting here is that the Pentagram was the Pythagorean sign for health, which is most appropriate.

Hexagram

The Hexagram which includes the hexagon and stands for the number six, is composed of two triangles. The upright Triangle of fire, which rises to heaven, a masculine, active symbol which is shown in the sprouting plant that forces its way through the ground and rises vertically in the air pointing to the sky; figuratively the aspirations of mankind.

The inverted Triangle is of water, which falls from the sky, and is pulled by the force of gravity to the lowest level, descending as rain, flowing into the seas as rivers and seeping into the ground. This is fresh water, unlike salt water, the sustaining moisture of all life, figuratively the emotions of creatures.

The male, positive, fire Triangle interlaced with the inverted female, negative, water Triangle, is the symbol of the unity of opposites in perfect harmony. This is therefore taken as the symbol of Spirit and Matter in harmonious accord.

We have found our triangles, cross and pentagrams, but where is the Hexagram? The sun rises or is born in the morning in the East, the Cross and the Pentagrams of the valley of Rennes les Bains symbolise this, 'awakening' or descent of Spirit into Matter. Within the Cross takes place the development of the five elements in the year, and the senses in man. this is youth and adolescence of man and woman. It grows to its greatest strength and height in the South at noon, which is the symbol of blossoming manhood and womanhood. From this height it declines and 'dies' or sets in the evening in the West, which is the symbol of old age and death, Rennes le Château being in the West, stands for the temple or tomb. This is the same as a circle of sacred stones on a hilltop, or King Solomon's Temple on a hillock, it is the place of harmony and wisdom, and of worship and thanksgiving. So the Hexagram is appropriate for Rennes le Château, and some have therefore tried to make out that it belongs to the otherwise plain armorial shield of this place. (In *Armorial Général*, 1876, Charles d'Hozier describes the shield 'of azure with a gold border'. I include however, the Hexagram on the cover of this book).

This Hexagram is therefore called the Shield of Solomon and the symbol of the Macrocosm. Thus Sunrise is the youth and aspiration of man, the Midday sun maturity and struggle, and Sunset old age and wisdom.

For our Piscean Age of Jesus we found that we had the constellation Pisces as the place of the vernal, and Virgo that of the autumn equinoxes, similarly Gemini for the summer, and Sagittarius for the winter solstices. As we know that the division of the zodiac into constellations had already become unequal at this time, we will therefore use the equal divisions of the signs as in Astrology, but beginning with the sign of Pisces instead of Aries, for this Age.

The Cross and its Zodiacal Signs

As we have found that our Cross represents sunset at the vernal equinox in Pisces, the sign of Pisces is just about to set on the western arm at the Homme Mort, and Virgo about to rise on the eastern arm of the source of the Madeleine, in the southern arm we have Gemini of the summer, and in the northern arm Sagittarius of the winter solstices.

Pentagram (First) and Signs

In this Pentagram we have the northern angle aligned with the axis of the Cross. Around it we have:

1	Arm of the Cross and Devil's Chair 270°	falls in Sagittarius.
1	Rennes le Château Church 340°. Maurine Spring 341^1/2°	falls in Aquarius.
1	le Bézu Church 51^1/2°. Jasse du Bézu 49^1/2°	falls in Aries.
1	Vialasse ruin 123^1/2°	falls in Cancer.
1	Soulane Hill 192^1/2°	falls in Virgo.

We will take this Pentagram as it is the only one to be directly connected to the Triangle, this is at the apex of Jasse du Bézu, and the church of Rennes le Château.

Hexagram and Signs

In the Hexagram we will orientate the apex of the upright Triangle to the East, and that of the inverted Triangle to the West. The Jewish Temple at Jerusalem and early Christian churches were oriented to the West, while later churches are generally oriented to the East, or if correctly aligned, to the sunrise on the Saint's Day to whom they are dedicated. So on our Hexagram we will put, in accord with our Cross, Virgo in the East, and Pisces in the West, and as there are six angles as points in our Hexagram, and 12 signs of the zodiac, we will put around it each alternate sign from Pisces and Virgo, anticlockwise in their order of rising as around our Cross. We now have Virgo in the East with Scorpio, Capricorn, Pisces, Taurus and Cancer around it. (See Fig. 20.)

124

Triangle and Signs

We now see that between our Hexagram, first Pentagram, and Cross, we have all the signs of the zodiac except Leo and Libra.

Leo the Lion

This is the summer sign when the kings of Babylon used to hunt the lions which ravaged the herds at watering places, especially in the summer drought. The ferocity and strength of the lion resembled the heat of the midsummer sun, thus the lion became the symbol of kings, like the Lion of Judah. The lion we will naturally put due South on the apex of our Triangle at le Bézu.

Libra the Scales

These originated with the weighing of the heart in the old Egyptian religion, when the dead appeared at the judgement of Osiris. The heart was weighed against a feather, representing Truth, if the good deeds were more than the bad, the soul was saved and went to heaven, but otherwise it was swallowed by a strange creature called Am-mit, whose fore was that of a crocodile, body of a lion and rear of a hippopotamus. This savage devourer whose fore and aft animals were creatures of Set the destroyer, and Sekhet's lion of the terrible midsummer sun, appears to represent to the three seasons of four months each in the ancient Egyptian year, or at least their unpleasant aspects.

The first is represented by the Crocodile, and stands for the rise of the Nile to the middle of autumn the period of the inundation, when this dangerous animal in early times came on to the land with the floods. The second period of the end of autumn, winter, and early spring, the time of growth, fertility being symbolised by Ta-urt a pregnant Hippo.

The last four months from late spring to the heliacal rising of Sothis and the beginning of the rise of the Nile, is the hot dry period of the Lion. This animal Am-mit therefore seems to be a symbol of reincarnation and rebirth in one of the seasons of the year.

Thus we can associate Libra with death and judgement in the West, and with Rennes le Château. Now what is the third zodiacal sign to be placed on the third angle of our Triangle at Rennes les Bains? Around the zodiac are in sequence: **Gemini**, Cancer, **Leo**, Virgo, **Libra**.

We have Leo and Libra. As our Triangle is equilateral, the distance from Bézu (Leo) to Rennes le Château (Libra) being the same as from Bézu (Leo) to Rennes les Bains the latter must be Gemini, also Gemini falls on the top arm of our Cross, in the valley of Rennes les Bains marking the summer solstice of the 'Fishes Age'.

The two solstices were called the 'Gates of the Sun', and writing in the 5th century, Macrobius informs us that the souls passed through the milky way and into the zodiac by the gate of Cancer. This of course takes Cancer to be the constellation of the summer solstice, which in our era is really Gemini. By this gate the souls also enter the Heavenly Triangle of the Holy Spirit and travel around the zodiac to the place of the autumn equinox (Virgo).

Here they take on the Cross of Spirit and Matter, and their bodies are formed by pentagrams of the elements. Judged (Libra), they 'fall', and proceed to their respective Signs to be born on Earth.

We see that our Triangle represents the daily path of the sun, rising in the East at Rennes les Bains, crossing the meridian at midday at le Bézu, and setting in the West at Rennes le Château.

In the year with the three zodiacal signs placed deasul to resemble the apparent movement of the sun, in the East (Rennes les Bains) Gemini, in the South (le Bézu) Leo, and in the West (Rennes le Château) Libra, we have the year from the summer solstice in Gemini, through to Libra here October - November.

The judgement of souls was at the end of the Celtic year. The Attic month Boedromion (September - October) is that of the Greater Mysteries of Eleusis, and the time of the autumn sowing with which they were connected. The sowing of wheat is in October in our part of Europe, and by the beginning of November we become aware of the effect of the sun descending into the lower hemisphere, thus it is more appropriate that Libra corresponding to October - November is placed here.

In our Triangle we have:

Location	Direction	Sign	Planet Day House
Rennes les Bains	East	Gemini	mercury
le Bézu	South	Leo	sun
Rennes le Château	West	Libra	venus

This is in accord with the idea that the Triangle represents the three positions of the sun, its rise, midday, and its setting.

We have here the two inner planets, which unlike the outer ones are to be seen nearer to the horizon before sunrise or after sunset, for the maximum elongation of mercury from the sun is 28° and that of venus 47°, thus their day houses are as close as possible to that of the sun.

Mercury, messenger of the gods has his planet in Gemini, linking the Triangle to the Cross in the valley of Rennes les Bains, and he is also appropriately the god of shepherds.

Similarly, that of Venus is present who is the goddess of the Sacred Grove, the Bethel on the mountain, or the temple, and of the mystery cults, here the church of Mary Magdalen at Rennes le Château.

The apex of our Triangle is to be found at le Bézu where the sun is at its highest and strongest, and his royal lion, Leo, but at this place there is not so much to be seen on the ground because here the sun in our Triangle is above the horizon. It is the most spiritual point. In the ensigns of the tribes of Israel, Leo is unquestionably that of Judah, the interpretations of some of the others vary, however, here we will accept that Libra belongs to Levi and Gemini to Benjamin. Thus:

Leo, sun, King, and House of Judah.

Libra the scales of judgement, which replaced the Chaldean Tulku, the Sacred Mound, or Holy Altar. This then is appropriate for the tribe of Levi, who became the priests of the Temple, here the sacred hill of Rennes le Château.

Gemini the twins, representing the male and female nature, solar and lunar, originating probably from the Babylonian Epic of the solar Gilgamesh and the lunar Eabani, hence Castor and Pollux. The tribe of Benjamin in the Blessings of Jacob was described as a wolf

126

devouring the prey in the morning and dividing the spoil at night, as the small dog Canis Minor is a paranatellon of the constellation Gemini, this may be the 'wolf', and the duality of morning and night also suggests the Twins.

The prophets of Israel belonged to the tribe of Benjamin, so here the valley of Rennes les Bains with the Cromlech of the Druids and the Cross is therefore appropriate.

Judges

Israel was ruled by a succession of Judges (who seemed to have resembled the Arch Druids) the twelfth and last of whom was Samuel. The people wanted a king, so he anointed Saul as king, and it is thought that he may have later anointed David. Samuel, and Saul the first king, belonged to the tribe of Benjamin. David who was born at Bethlehem of the tribe of Judah, deposed King Saul and himself became King of Israel, thus he deprived the Benjaminites of the throne in favour of Judah, and established his capital in Jerusalem which he took from the Jebusites who were a remnant of the Canaanites. Jerusalem then became the site of worship of Jehovah, thus providing the site of King Solomon's Temple.

The Figures

If we look at the diagrams (Fig 20) we see the Triangle of Pure Spirit represented by Bézu and the two Rennes, which is that of the tribes of Judah, Benjamin, and Levi, or of Kings, Prophets and Priests.

The souls descend from heaven by the Gate of the summer solstice, which is Gemini in the Piscean era, and into the Cross of Spirit embodied in matter, or the World. They take on the first Pentagram of the five elements of the Microcosmic Man crucified on the cross. Thus in the Holy Valley we have the symbolic evolution of man, but when he climbs the Holy Mountain, represented by Rennes le Château, there he commences the Great Work which is to change the Hexagram from its negative to its positive aspect.

The Moon and the night mansions of the planets as rulers of the elements, have to be changed into the day houses of the Sun. When this is accomplished the first Pentagram of the Moon (as the Mind) and the night of darkness of early Religions is changed into the Second of the Sun (as Love) and Light of the Christian Church, it is the work of the axis of Spirit. Then the Soul passes the Judgement of his deeds (Libra), has a united heart and mind devoted to God (Gemini), and through his striving and the strength of His Grace (Leo), he ascends to Heaven as symbolised by the Triangle.

- He was Purified in the east at Rennes les Bains, and Enthroned.
- Consecrated in the west at Rennes le Château, and Anointed.
- Raised on the Meridian at le Bézu, and Crowned.

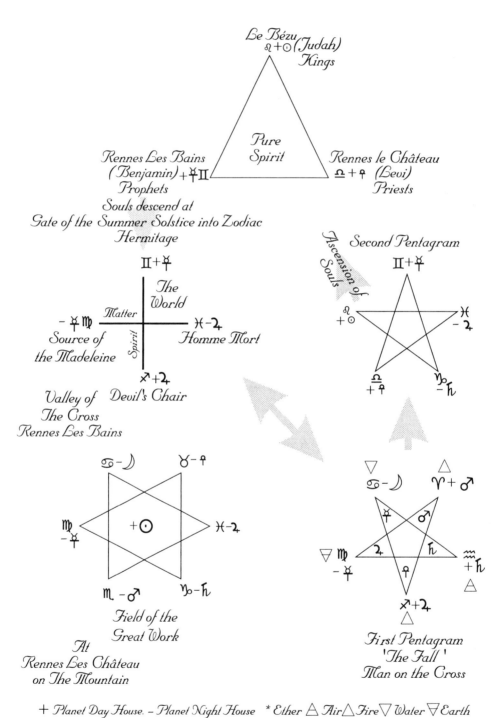

Le Bézu
♌+☉ (Judah)
Kings

Pure
Spirit

Rennes Les Bains
(Benjamin) +☿♊
Prophets

Rennes le Château
♎ + ♀ (Levi)
Priests

Souls descend at
Gate of the Summer Solstice into Zodiac
Hermitage

♊+☿

The
World

Matter

- ☿ ♍   ♓ -♃
Source of   Homme Mort
the Madeleine

Spirit

♐+♃

Valley of   Devil's Chair
The Cross
Rennes Les Bains

Second Pentagram
♊+☿

Ascension of
Souls

♌
+☉   ♓
-♃

♎   ♑
+♀   -♄

♋-☽   ♉-♀

♍
-☿   +☉   ♓-♃

♏ -♂   ♑-♄

Field of the
Great Work

At
Rennes Les Château
on The Mountain

▽   △
♋-☽   ♈+♂

☿   ♂

▽ ♍   ♃   ♄   ♒
-☿   +♄

♀   △

♐+♃
△

First Pentagram
'The Fall '
Man on the Cross

+ Planet Day House. − Planet Night House   * Ether △ Air △ Fire ▽ Water ▽ Earth

Fig. 20. Figures and Attributes.

In the diagram (Fig. 21) we see this negative Hexagram of the 'world' in darkness, which is that of the First Degree and the Neophyte. This is composed of the trine of the element Earth, Virgo, Taurus and Capricorn; and also that of Water, Cancer, Scorpio and Pisces. It is probably this Hexagram which is depicted in the Greek myth where Hephaestus (the God of Fire and Metallic Arts, the Latin Vulcanus) forged a net, then, when he caught his unfaithful wife Aphrodite (the Goddess of Love, both profane and pure, the Latin Venus) in passionate embrace with Ares (the hero god, Latin Mars), he threw this net over them to their great discomfort, and the laughter of all the other gods.

In the Second Degree, which belongs to the feminine aspect of our nature, the trine of Earth is changed by the action of Venus (Aphrodite, whose sphere of action was in the elements Earth, Water and Air) into the Air trine, Gemini, Libra and Aquarius, this is shown by the fact that the planet of Venus has the furthest distance to travel, from its night house in Taurus to its day house in Libra.

This work represents the change of heart in the candidate from the desire for sex and worldly things, to pure love and the gifts of the Spirit. Aphrodite (Venus) was the goddess of Marriage, and of Spring, this Degree therefore represents the Lesser Mysteries that were held at this time.

The work here is that of taming the Bull (Taurus) so that it will draw the plough; or the labour, devotion, and self-sacrifice, involved in bringing up a family.

In the Third Degree, that of the Greater Mysteries and of death and the harvest, Mars for the same reason, changes the Water trine, Cancer, Scorpio and Pisces, into the Fire trine, Leo, Sagittarius and Aries. This symbolises the struggle of the higher mind (Fire) to control the base instincts and emotions (Water).

The Hexagram has been changed from that of darkness into that of light, and it now points to the South (instead of the East) where at midday the sun is at its highest on the meridian, and at the top of this Hexagram are Libra, Leo and Gemini, which with their intermediary night houses, form the sky, or the upper hemisphere.

When Leo is crossing the meridian in day time, then Scorpio is beginning to rise in the East and Taurus about to set in the West, but we cannot see them, here is the traditional opposition which we have already seen in the myths.

These top three Signs of the Hexagram of the Third Degree are part of it, however, when raised to the Royal (Leo) Arch of Heaven, they give us those of the Triangle of Spirit.

We see however, that in our Triangle, Gemini (now at Rennes les Bains) has changed place with Libra (now at Rennes le Château). This is because in the first Hexagram we have the apparent movement of the stars at night, in a clockwise manner around the sky, the sun also appears to move in the same manner from its rise to its set. The observer knows however from the constellations which it passes through, that the sun seems to be moving in an anticlockwise manner around the zodiac, but this is inadmissible, everyone knows that 'the sun moves from East to West', hence the term 'Deasul' (with the sun) for clockwise perambulations. Anticlockwise or 'Widdershins' was thought to be evil, and against nature, the movement of witches, so the sun is shown here with the Signs that are depicted in a clockwise order, thus Gemini has been allocated to the East and Libra to the West. In the

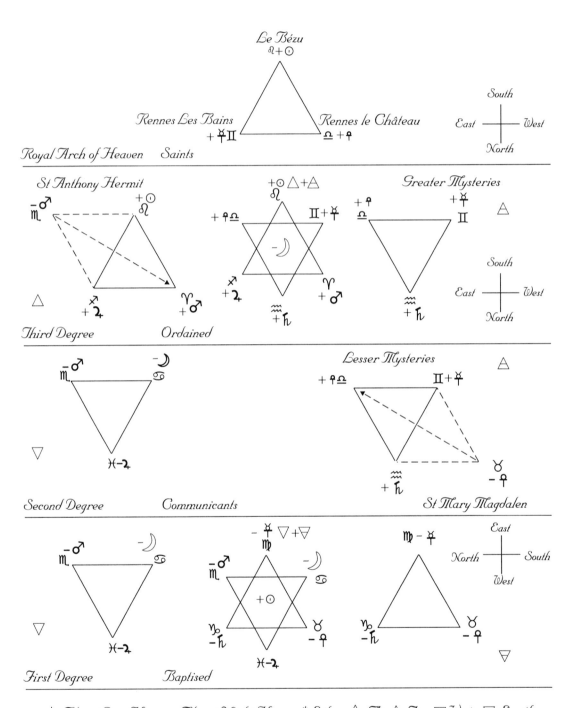

Fig. 21. Changing the Hexagram.

+ Planet Day House. – Planet Night House   * Ether △ Air △ Fire ▽ Water ▽ Earth

130

church of Rennes le Château are St Mary Magdalen, who has the qualities of Venus and represents the Second Degree, whilst St Anthony, who struggled against the temptations of the devils, corresponds to Mars and the Third Degree. But to whom belongs the First Degree? Clearly to the repentant Devil under the stoup!

In the Christian Church these four Degrees in the diagram represent:

1   The World — and the Baptised.
2   The Body of the Church — and the Communicants.
3   The Resurrection — and the Ordained.
4   The Ascension — and the Saints.

The Circle and the Cross

In *La Vraie Langue Celtique*, the Reverend Boudet describes how he found 'Greek' crosses carved on various stones situated in his 'Cromlech' of the Valley of Rennes les Bains. It is very difficult today to explore these sights as they are so over-grown with scrub, and nobody has written a book verifying these crosses, there is one however which is easily reached on the rocking stone, 'La Roche Tremblante' near the Devil's Chair, and if one climbs a little way on to the stone, it is then clearly visible on its upper surface.

Boudet claims that these were carved by early Christians to convert the pagan site, this phenomenon is also to be found elsewhere where Greek crosses have been engraved on menhirs and other pagan sacred stones. Perhaps he was also hinting at the 'Cross' of the Valley which we have discovered?

The pagans held their fairs, which were also occasions for judgements, betrothals and weddings, trade etc. as we have seen, near their barrows or burial ground christianised by the presence of an anchorite's cell or an Oratory, and later a churchyard cross.

This then 'crossed', the pagan circle, and from this when carved in stone arose the Celtic Cross, the Cross that the Visigoths laid out in our valley converted it from a pagan circle (Boudet's Cromlech), into a Christian site.

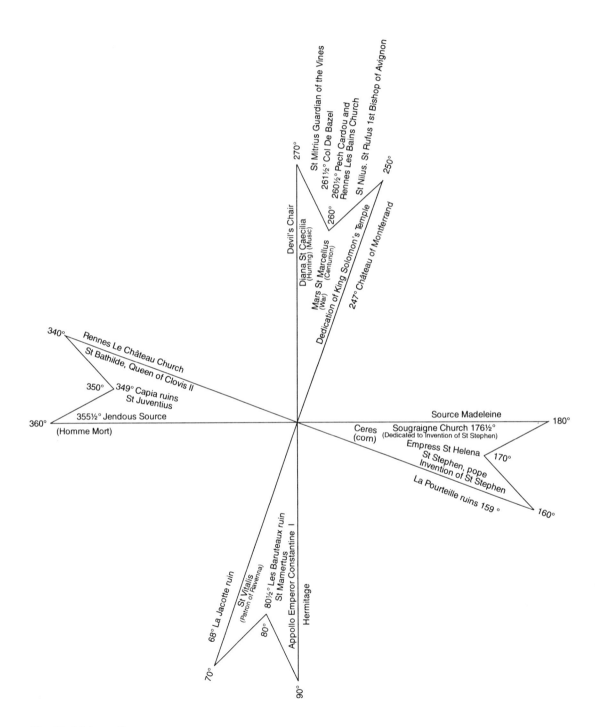

Fig. 22. Maltese Cross.

132

Maltese Cross or the Cross of the Eight Beatitudes

If one takes the alignments of our Cross and place another cross 20° East of its northern arm, with the same centre, one then has the arms of a Maltese Cross. The alignments are:

360° -4^1/$_2$° = 355^1/$_2$°	Jendous Source Captée. (See Third Pentagram.)
340°	Rennes le Château. St Bathilde the Merovingian Queen. (See First Pentagram.)
270°	Devil's Chair. Diana, goddess of hunting. St Caecilia, patron of music. (See First Pentagram.)
250° -3° = 247°	Château of Montferrand. Mars, god of war. St Marcellus the Christian centurion martyr. Dedication of King Solomon's Temple. (See Fourth Pentagram.)
180°	Source de la Madeleine. Fontaine des Amours. Ceres, goddess of corn. SS Claudius, Asterius, etc. (See Fourth Pentagram.)
160° - 1° = 159°	La Pourteille ruins. 1st August Lugnasad. St Peter in chains. (2nd August St Stephen, pope, martyr.) (3rd August Invention of St Stephen.) (See Second Pentagram.)
90°	Hermitage. Apollo, god. Emperor Constantine the Great. (See Second Pentragram.)
70° - 2° = 68°	La Jacotte ruins. 28th April. St Vitalis, martyr, patron of Ravenna. (See Third Pentagram.)

We see that the male vertical axis of this Maltese Cross has at its base the rather masculine Diana, goddess of hunting, and Mars god of war, aptly there is also St Marcellus the Christian Roman Centurion martyr, and the Château of Montferrand.

At the top of the Cross is Apollo god of the sun which is at its highest when it crosses the meridian, it symbolises the position of kings set high above their vassals, and is suitable, bearing in mind Constantine's devotion to Apollo, for the Emperor saw the cross above the midday sun, and after his victory at Rome founded the established Christian Church.

Thus our Maltese Cross as well as incorporating our Cross, is connected with all four pentagrams.

Intermediary Alignments

To make this Saltire cross into a Maltese cross of eight points we need four extra markers and the nearest are:

350° - 1° = 349° Capia ruins. 8th February.
> *St Juventius, bishop of Pavia, 2nd century AD.*

St Juventius was sent to Milan to comfort the local Christians after the martydom of St Nazaire and St Celse there. Thus this saint is of local interest.

260° + 1/2° = 2601/2° Pech Cardou peak. Rennes les Bains Church.
> *12th November. St Nilus. St Rufus, first bishop of Avignon.*
> *13th November. St Mitrius (see following marker).*

It is remarkable that our alignment here passes through both the site of the church and also the peak of the high hill of Cardou above, thus linking the mountain to the church by the riverside. In the area of our Cross, the river Blanque, obviously named after the Great Mother in her aspect of the White Goddess and the Moon, flows roughly from the South to the North, joining the river Sals just before Rennes les Bains which also continues to the North. This is roughly in line with our Cross from the alignment to the Hermitage and that to the Devil's Chair, and beyond.

It was because the Nile flowed from the South to the North like the Milky Way that the Ancient Egyptians named the latter the 'Celestial Nile', and considered them to be sacred, likewise in India the Ganges which flows to the East, turns North at Benares for a short distance making this town particularly sacred. The Milky Way crosses the constellations between Scorpio and Sagittarius in the South and again between Taurus and Gemini in the North, likewise the Maltese cross is bounded here by the alignment to La Jacotte ruins at 68° or 8° into the sign of Taurus and the Hermitage at 90° and 1° of Gemini. The North of this Cross is in the same manner marked by the Château of Montferrand 247° or 7° into the sign of Scorpio and the Devil's Chair 270° and the 1st degree of Sagittarius.

Though the signs here happen to have the opposite orientation to those of the constellations, it nevertheless clearly ties the River of Heaven to our river and its Holy Valley, and it is therefore very befitting to have St Nilus here.

The most remarkable thing about this alignment is that it is exactly at 260°, the middle axis of the Maltese cross and is hence linked to the church of St Nazaire and Celse at Rennes les Bains.

We ought to mention here:

+1° = 2611/2° Col de Bazel, peak. 13 November.
> *St Mitrius (Merre), Patron of Aix in Provence, guardian of the vines,*
> *304 AD.*

St Merre is of local interest and the Col de Bazel towers immediately above Rennes les Bains.

170° + 6¹/₂° = 176¹/₂° Sougraigne Church 19th August.
> *'The Apparition of the Cross' to the Emperor Constantine.*
> *20th August Samuel, prophet. St Amator, servant of the Virgin Mary.*
> *(St Louis, Bishop of Toulouse, 1295 AD.)*
> *(18th August. St Helena, mother of Constantine.)*

The eve of the day of this marker is the day of St Helena the Christian mother of the Emperor Constantine who adopted the Chi-Rho cross, and it was claimed that she discovered the true Cross of Christ. The 19th is the day commemorating Constantine's vision of this Chi-Rho cross over the midday sun. These memorials are very suitable for the early Church, and the connection of Galla Placidia with the region and the cross. Sougraigne Church is dedicated to the Invention of St Stephen. This arm of the Maltese cross is bounded by the marker of La Pourteille ruins and St Peter in chains which is 1° from the ideal alignment of 160°. One degree on the other side however, would fall within the arm of the Cross and gives us the memorial of the 'Invention of St Stephen' which is very apt.

80° + ¹/₂° = 80¹/₂° les Baruteax ruin. 11th May.
> *St Mamertus, bishop of Vienne, 477 AD.*
> *12th May St Epiphanius, bishop, 403 AD.*

We have already seen how St Mamertus instituted the Rogation days when he was bishop of Vienne in the South of France, which has about the same latitude as both the Rennes and also Ravenna, thus this saint is very relevant here.

The Maltese cross that we have found contains many of our important alignments and is therefore of great interest.

Knights Templar

Fig. 23. Knights Templar Figures.

The Knights Templar formed a Commandery in Campagne sur Aude in 1244, and at the Bézu towards the end of the 13th century. This is thought to have been where the Bézu village is now, though its exact location is not known. It would appear that the Knights Templar knew about the traditions of our Triangle and the Valley of the Cross. As is well known, the Seal of the Order of the Temple had two knights riding a single horse, holding a lance. This represents their poverty, but also can be taken to mean the twins Gemini above (the summer solstice), the lance and horse or the archer Centaur, Sagittarius, (the winter solstice) constellations of the Piscean Age. These then stand for the vertical arm of the Cross, the horizontal arm is implied by their special devotion to the Virgin Mary as Virgo, and the rule that they had to eat fish three times a week, for Pisces.

On the ancient boundary stones of the fields in Chaldea were inscribed three stars, each within a circle, representing the Trinity of Sin the moon god, Shamash the sun god and Ishtar the goddess of venus, these form a triad of our Triangle in the Aries Era. (With the summer solstice in Cancer house of the moon instead of in Gemini, the sun in Leo, and venus in Libra.)

Probably the knowledge concerning the relation of the zodiacal signs to the Pythagorean figures was known to the Knights Templar, for at Carentoir in Morbihan, Brittany, there was a Commandery and there still exists the church dedicated to St John of the Temple. Used as a lintel over the fireplace in a house in the town is a most interesting stone which originally belonged to the Templars. We have a rectangular frame of double lines within which on the right is a pentagram in a circle, on the left is a hexagram also in a circle and in the middle a diamond in which is engraved the initials C B S P which probabaly stands for: *Carentoir, Bretagne,* and *S P* for *Seigneurie* (manor) *Principale, Sainte Preiuré* (priory) or even *Saint Peter.* (See Fig. 23.)

This confirms the figures around our Triangle, taking the top to be the North, it gives a pentagram to the East (Rennes les Bains), and a hexagram to the West (Rennes le Château). In the middle is a diamond, within which are the initials of their Commandery, which figure would belong here to le Bézu, but a diamond is a four sided figure, and really belongs to the Cross at Rennes les Bains, so what should be here? When two circles of equal diameter intersect their arcs produce a pointed oval, a line joining their centres cuts this in two places. If one joins these four points of intersection it produces a lozenge, thus the diamond comes

136

forth from the oval. An oval is therefore formed from two circles, but a circle or oval is the symbol of the heavens (like the zodiac and its ecliptic) and not a linear figure like those we have allotted to the two Rennes, it therefore belongs to the meridian above le Bézu.

Probably because the Templars domain was on earth, like le Bézu, they substituted a lozenge for the oval. When the sun has just set in Gemini at the summer solstice (Piscean era),Virgo is to be seen crossing the meridian. We have identified the latter constellation with the Virgin Mary, Mary Magdalen, Ceres, and indirectly Isis and Hathor. Thus the souls which have entered the zodiac by the gate of the summer solstice at midday, at sunset take on materiality at the horizontal axis of the Cross, then they are 'born' from the Great White Mother, or Virgin, represented by Virgo at its highest elevation on the meridian.

So le Bézu was rightly named Albedunum White (Alba) Fort (Dunum), after the White Goddess. These souls are later born from their physical mother at the allotted time. The universal symbol of birth is the pointed Oval, representing the pudendum, this is depicted by the Almond and the Vesica Piscis, the emblems of the 'Queens of Love' and of 'Heaven'.

In the sacred place of Luz (almond), Jacob set up his Pillar stone (a masculine symbol), and renamed the site *Bethel* (Hebrew for 'House of God'), he thereby changed it from a place of Goddess worship, to that of God. (Jacob, Hebrew *Yaqobh*, is thought to mean 'supplanter'). He was the father of the 12 Patriarchs of Israel, and clearly belongs here to the Holy Valley of Rennes les Bains. Moses, whose alignment we found in the first Pentagram, as leader, lawgiver and the exemplary Prophet, is also here; but his brother Aaron, the first High Priest and Levite, who had a rod that gave almonds (Numbers XVII 8), therefore belongs to Rennes le Château. It is interesting here that Aaron in Hebrew means 'lofty', 'mountainous'.

The levites, priests of Israel, did not have a zodiacal constellation of their own, for their place was in the centre of the Encampment, with the Twelve Tribes around it, which each had a symbol representing a constellation of the zodiac on its banner, and here they belong to the Cross at Rennes les Bains. The Levites, being the priests, here belong to Rennes le Château for worship in the Temple on the Holy Mountain. St Mary Magdalen (*Magdala* is Greek for 'Almond'. There the doves for sacrifice in the Temple were bred), to whom the church is dedicated, is the prime example of transmuting desire for earthly love to that of the Spirit (the two aspects of Venus). This is the act of 'raising' the soul from the horizontal axis to that of the vertical one in the Cross. Thus through her example as the supreme penitent, contemplating alone the Saviour in the 'cave' of the heart (symbolised by La Sancte Baume), the Christian hopes to regain the Kingdom of Heaven above, here figuratively above le Bézu.

Macrobius also informs us (Som. Scip. 1,12) that the souls who are able, ascend after death by the Gate of the Gods, and become immortal gods themselves.

The soul is born again of Spirit through the Son of God, which is symbolised by the birth of Jesus who being sinless, entered the world by the Gate of the Gods, at midnight on the winter solstice. Then, Macrobius tells us, the day being short the sun god was therefore compared to a feeble child. At this time the sun is at its lowest on the meridian, and in the bottom of the 'underworld' from where it will rise and ascend again on the meridian. Thus when the moment comes for the soul to be born again, the individual Spirit enters the world at this period by the Gate of the Gods, to join its soul and elevate it, in order to become also a son of God.

In the Piscean era, the constellation Virgo is on the eastern horizon when the sun is in that of Sagittarius at midnight of the winter solstice. As the sun in Sagittarius rises to be 'born' at daybreak so also Virgo ascends to cross the meridian, she is the Queen of Heaven, and being identified with her, so also are the Virgin Mary (in Hebrew 'Miriam'), Ceres and Isis etc.

The story of the Israelites being led out of Egypt (called *Khem* black, after its alluvial Nile soil) has been taken to depict the lifting of the souls from Darkness (Egypt) into Light, (Israel, our 'Alba'), their leaders were Moses (here at Rennes les Bains), Aaron (here at Rennes le Château) and Miriam their sister. So Miriam (our Mary) clearly belongs to the Heavens above le Bézu.

It is interesting to observe that whilst St Caecilia, the Patron Saint of Music and Harmony, is here at the bottom of our Cross in the Holy Valley, Miriam who led the children of Israel in music, song and dance, (Exod. XV 20 - 21) is at the apex of the Triangle.

The Christian is symbolically:

- Baptised at Rennes les Bains in the Holy Valley.
- Confirmed at Rennes le Château on the Holy Mountain.
- Communes with the Company of Heaven above le Bézu, through participating in the Blessed Sacrament.

Templarii

Alfred Weysen in his second book about the zodiac which he found in the area of the gorges of Verdon points out that it is bounded by nine chapels whose saints' initials spell out 'TEMPLARII' (*Le Temple du Secret et l' Apocalypse* p.36) which are:

T rophime
É tienne
M aur
P ierre
L aurent
A nne
R och
I (J) ulien
I (J) ean

He states "The treasure [zodiac] of the Templars of the region was signed". Without this brilliant deduction I would never have thought of looking at our own area for this, which has:

T — —-
É tienne, invention of. (Sougraigne)
M ary Magdalen. (Rennes le Château), Michael. (Coustaussa.) Martin. (Cassaignes.) Mary. Assumption of the Virgin (Bugarach)
P eter in chains. (Serres.)
L eocadia. (Luc sur Aude)
A nne. (Arques)
R — —
I (J) ohn Baptist. (Couiza)
I (J) ohn Baptist. (Le Bézu)

138

These are the early towns or villages dating from Visigothic times. But how do we get the T and the R? Also, I am not happy about the R in the list of Verdon chapels because the Order of the Temple was dissolved in 1312 AD and St Roch died in 1327. If, as is most likely, this was arranged in concordance with the Templars and Ecclesia, then we would not have a chapel dedicated to St Roch.

What then do our T and R stand for? Obviously Terra Rhedarum! Both 'signatures' have SS Étienne, Pierre and Anne in common; and in the case of the letter M, we have a female saint in either place. T R can also stand for Terra Regis, as the holy place of the 'Kingdom' of God on earth.

T, the last letter called *Tau* ('cross') of the Hebrew alphabet, and has the form of the Egyptian cross of Life which is that of St Anthony the hermit, who is so closely connected with our valley, and was remembered at the Bugarach pageant (*Tau* is the sign of 'Life'). T is the 22nd letter in Hebrew, and the 22nd letter of the Greek alphabet as we have seen is Chi, and R, Rho is the 17th; thus T suggests the Cross, and T and R, Chi and Rho, the first two letters of Christos, and the Chi Rho-Cross. So the Cross of the Valley of the Cross is implied here!

Pentagram

The five saints between the Terra Rhedarum therefore give us a pentagram, headed by St Étienne, (Greek for 'Crown') the protomartyr (St Stephen).

The memorials of our saints here:

- Étienne, invention. 3rd August.
- Mary Magdalen. 22nd of July.
- Peter in chains. 1st of August.
- Leocadia. 9th December.
- Anne. 26th of July.

Except that of St Leocadia, all of these fall between the 22nd of July and the 3rd of August, 13 days in all, which include the first decan of the sign of Leo, beginning on the 23rd of July. Astrologically, Leo a day mansion is ruled by the Sun, and its first decan, though it has in theory the sub-ruler Saturn, is completely controlled by the Sun, and gives the purest Leo type of the three decans of this sign. Leo, the time of year when the sun is strongest, is the symbol of Rulers and in the constellation its chief star *Regulus* means a 'King'.

The 22nd, as we have discovered, is the beginning of the second half of our Druidic Year, and the beginning of the Sothic year of ancient Egypt. This of course symbolises the Height of Heaven that the Christians want to bring about on earth, and here the Holy Land of Rhedae, the Valley of the Cross and the Triangle of the Holy Trinity.

Near Couiza is the village of Montazels which grew up around an ancient monastery. This being desolate was turned into a château by a Noble called d'Hautpoul, to whom it was given by Viscount Bernard Aton at the beginning of the 11th century. His descendants became the last Lords of Rennes le Château. The present church is dedicated to St Caecilia, which may have taken its name from this monastery. Now we have seen how Couiza at 330° marks the 20th of January when the sun enters the sign of Aquarius, suprisingly enough Montazels at

333° corresponds to the 23rd, the first day of the Druidic Year. As I am uncertain of its age, I did not include this monastery with the churches, though it may well date back to Visigothic times. In the Alternative Arrangement it would mark the 31st of May of St Petronilla the supposed daughter of St Peter.

There at Montazels the Reverend Saunière was born. So here we have it! Not only is our area signed by the TEMPLARII, but also this church is dedicated to the Saint to whom the Northern arm of our Cross is aligned in the calendar.

Tomb and ruin of Pontils. 254° 6th November. St Leonard, patron of prisoners

Some think that this tomb was depicted in Poussin's painting of The Shepherds of Arcadia, and therefore dates from the 17th century or earlier, which suits their theories. Pierre Jarnac (Les Archives II p 383) claims that this was built for Jean Galibert in 1903 by the mason Bourriel of Rennes les Bains. In either case its alignment being so close to that of the Ancient Mine on the slopes of the Col de Bazel 256°, and its memorial of the Four Crowned Martyrs, patrons of the Guilds of Stonemasons, clearly indicates that some Freemasons knew about our Cross, the 'Tomb' is also particularly relevant. Was Jean Galibert a Freemason, and did he learn about our Cross from Saunière?

St Leonard is appropriate here as patron of prisoners, for nearby on one side is Serres church, dedicated to St Peter in chains, and on the other is that of Arques of St Anne. We have already noted the possibility of there having been at Arques a Black Virgin, one of whose characteristics was to release prisoners.

Conclusion

And so we arrive at the end of this book.

- We have followed the clues of the Abbé Saunière and found the Inverted Cross oriented to the South in our Holy Valley of Rennes les Bains.

- We have found how the various features, such as springs, ruins, peaks, churches and castles were aligned to it in order to highlight some memorial in the calendar that is superimposed upon it.

- We have discovered the perfect equilateral Triangle of le Bézu and the two Rennes, the Cross, the Five Pentagrams and the Hexagram of Rennes le Château.

- We have discussed the hypothesis that the Roman Princess, Empress, and Visigothic Queen, Galla Placidia visited the Valley of the Cross and was influenced by what she learnt there.

- We have recalled the traditions of the Celtic Church, and how they were suppressed by its rival the Roman Church.

- We have revealed something about the pre-Christian gods and goddesses which were connected with our Valley.

- We have discovered a secret of the Cathars, and the Druidic Year which has never before been openly discussed.

- We have found the undisclosed secrets of the Microcosmic Man and Woman, and how they are connected with the Pentagrams.

- We have disclosed the relationship of the Great Goddess with Arques and the neighbouring region.

- We have seen how the sign of the Zodiac and their planets have been placed around our Pythagorean figures, for the Piscean Era.

- Apart from Alan Leo who, in *Esoteric Astrology*, has shown how the Signs are placed around the Hexagram for the Aries Era, I have never before come across anything about these details revealed in Our Cross.

- We have seen how the Maltese Cross was formed from our Cross in the Holy Valley with its interesting alignments, and discussed the secret about the Figures left to us by the Knights Templar.

Have we not found the Gold of Wisdom, rather than the material substance discovered with metal detectors, and the reason for the absurd burrowings that have taken place at Rennes le Château and in the area?

This is not the treasure of the Gnomes, but that of the Two Salamanders!

French Bibliography

Alibcrt, Louis. *Dictionnaire Occitan Français* Institut d'Études Occitanes. Toulouse 1966
Bonvin, Jacques. *Vierges Noires*. Dervy Livres. Paris. 1989
Boudet, Henri. *La Vraie Langue Celtique*. 1886 (reprint Pierre Belfond. Paris 1978)
Boumendil, Claude.& Tappa, Gilbert. *Rennes le Château l'Église, Tu le vaincras.* Belisane 1983
Boumendil, Claude.& Tappa, Gilbert. *Les Cahiers de Rennes le Château* Belisane
Danis, J. C. *Toulouse Capitale Mystique*. L'Adret. St Gaudens 1985
Dumontier, M., Villeroux, N., Bernage, G., Barreau,T., *Sur les pas des Templiers en Bretagne, Normandie, Pays de Loire*. Henri Veyrier. Copernic 1986
Doumayrou, Guy René. *L'Esprit des Lieux* Centre International de Documentation Occitane. Béziers 1987
Eydoux, Henri Paul. *Promenades dans la France Antique* Plon. Paris. 1965.
Fabre, Albert. *Histoire d'Arques* Carcassonne 1885. (Philippe Schrauben reprint)
Fédié, Louis. *Comté de Razès* Carcassonne 1880 (Philippe Schrauben reprint)
Fourie, Jean. *Rennes le Château* L'Histoire de Rennes le Château, antérieure à 1789. Espéraza 1984
Jarnac, Pierre. *Histoire du Trésor de Rennes le Château* Cabestany 1985
Jarnac, Pierre. *Les Archives de Rennes le Château* Tome 1 & 2. Belisane 1987, 1988
Jaud, L. *Vies des Saints* Tours.
Lierre, Yves. *Le Secret des Prêtres du Razès, ou le mystère des deux Rennes* Neustrie. Caen 1986
Lobet, Marcel. *Histoire mystérieuse et tragique des Templiers* Soledi. Liège 1944
Marie, Franck. *La résurrection du Grand Cocu* S.R.E.S. Bagneux 1981
Mazières, Maurice René. 'Les Templiers du Bézu' extract from the Mémoires de la Société des Arts et des Sciences de Carcassonne. Tome 3. 4th serie.
Mazières, Maurice René & Monts, Bruno de. *Rennes le Château son histoire, ses seigneurs, ses curés, sa légende du trésor* Carcassonne 1982
Moula, D. F., & Sese, F. *Les deux Rennes; 1956 - 1976 l'affaire Saunière; 1884 - 1984 le mystère Boudet* Saint Severin 1984
Rivière, Jacques. *Le Fabuleux Trésor de Rennes le Château* Belisane 1983
Robin, Jean. *Rennes le Château la colline envoûtée* Guy Trédaniel 1982
Salverte, Eusebe. *Les Sciences Occultes* vol.I Paris 1829
Sède, Gérard de. *Le Trésor Maudit de Rennes le Château* J'ai Lu Paris
Sède, Gérard de. *Rennes le Château - Le dossier, les impostures, les phantasmes, les hypothèses* Robert Laffont. Paris 1988
Simonnet, P. B. *Réalité de la Magie et des Apparitions* Paris 1819
Weysen, Alfred. *Le Temple du Secret et L'Apocalypse* Robert Laffont 1990

English Bibliography

Encyclopaedia of Religion & Ethics James Hastings. T. & T. Clark. Edinburgh 1910
The Century Cyclopaedia of Names Benjamin Smith ed. The Times. London & NY 1904
Allen, J. Romilly. 'Christian Symbolism in Great Britain' Rhind lecture for 1885. London 1887
Allen, R. H. *Star Names* Dover Publications NY 1963
Baigent, M., Leigh, R., Lincoln, H. *The Holy Blood & the Holy Grail* Jonathan Cape 1982
Barclay, Edgar. *Stonehenge & its Earthworks* B. Nutt. London 1895
Bayley, Harold. *Archaic England* Chapman Hall 1919
Bayley, Harold. *The Lost Language of Symbolism* vol.2 Williams & Norgate
Blake, J. F. *Astronomical Myths* based on *Flammarion's History of the Heavens* Macmillan 1877
Blavatsky, H. P. *The Secret Doctrine* vol.2 1913
Blavatsky, H. P. *The Esoteric Character of the Gospels* Lucifer vol.1 reprint Int. Pub. House. Bombay
Bonwick, James. *Irish Druids & Old Irish Religions* R. Huddleston 1894
Bovini, Guiseppe. *Ravenna, its Mosaics & Monuments* L.O.S.A.R.P. Ravenna
Brady, John. *Clavis Calendaria* vol.1,2 London 1812
Budge, E. A. Wallis. *The Gods of the Egyptians* Methuen. London 1904
Bullinger, E. W. *Witness of the Stars* Eyre & Spottiswoode 1921
Burckhardt, Titus. *Alchemy* trans. from German by W. Stoddart. Stuart & Watkins London 1967
Carrington, Hereward. *Higher Psychical Development* K. Paul T. & T. London 1920
Carter, Frederick. *The Dragon of Revelation* Desmond & Harmsworth 1931
Chambers, R. *The Book of Days* vol.1& 2. W. R. Chambers. London & Edinburgh 1938
Chaplin, D. *Mythological Bonds between East & West*
Cornish, F. Warre, *Concise Dictionary of Greek & Roman Antiquities* John Murray. London 1898
Cox, M. R. *An Introductlon to Folklore* D. Nutt 1895
Crow, W. B. *The Calendar, Mysteries of the Ancients* No 7. Michael Houghton. London 1943
Crow, W. B. *Druids & the Mistletoe Sacrament, Mysteries of the Ancients* No 14 Michael Houghton London 1943
Cutts, E. L. *History of Early Christian Art* Soc. P. C. K. London 1893
Davies, Edward. *Celtic Researches* London 1804
Farbridge, M. H. *Studies in Biblical & Semitic Symbolism* Kegan, Paul, T. & T. 1923
Fellows, J. *The Mysteries of Freemasonry* Reeves & Turner 1877
French, F. *Prehistoric Faith & Worship* D. Nutt. 1912
Fortune, Dion. *The Mystical Qabalah* Williams & Norgate 1935
Garner, J. *The Worship of the Dead* Chapman Hall 1904
Goldsmith, Elizabeth, E. *Life Symbols as Related to Sex Symbolism* 1924
Bothwell-Gosse, A. *Craftsman & Saint* vol.8.The Comason. London 1916

Bothwell-Gosse, A. *The Magic Tree* vol.15. The Comason. London

Gould, S. Baring. *Curious Myths of the Middle Ages* Rivingtons. Oxford & Cambridge 1881

Gould, S. Baring. *Lives of the Saints* new ed. 16 vols. John. C. Nimmo. London 1898

Hall, Manley. P. 'Lectures on Ancient Philosophy'. 1923

Hawkins, Gerald. S., Rosenthal, Shoshana, K. *5,000 & 10,000 Year Star Catalogues* Smithsonian Contributions to Astrophysics Vol.10. No.2. Simthsonian Institute. Washington 1964

Hayes, Will. *The Book of the Cow* Dublin 1930

Hewitt, J. F. *Primitive Traditional History* vol.2. J. Parker. London 1907

Higgins, Godfrey. *Anacalypsis* vol.1 1833

Hone, William. *The Every-Day Book & Table Book* vol.1 London 1839

Hooper, Ivy. 'The Cele De or Culdees' vol.27 No. 162. *The Theosophical Review* Theosophical Publishing Society. London 1901

Inman, Thomas. *On Ancient Pillar Stones & Crosses* 1867

James, E. O. *Christian Myth & Ritual* John Murray 1933

James, E. O. *Seasonal Feasts & Festivals* Thames & Hudson 1961

Jobes, Gertrude & James. *Outer Space* The Scarecrow Press. London & NY 1964

Jowett, George. F. *The Drama of the Lost Disciples* Covenant Pub. Co. London 1961

Joyce, Donovan. *The Jesus Scroll* Angus Robertson. London 1973

Keightley,Thomas. *History of the Roman Empire* London 1850

King, C. W. *The Gnostics & Their Remains* 2nd ed. D. Nutt 1887

Krupp, E. C. (ed.) *In Search of Ancient Astronomies* Chatto & Windus. London 1979

Lassus, Jean. *The Early Christian & Byzantine World* Paul Hamlyn. London 1967

Lethbridge, T. C. *Witches* Routledge & Kegan Paul. London

Lewis, Lionel. S. *Glastonbury The Mother of Saints* 2nd ed. A. W. M. 1927

Lewis, Lionel. S. *St Joseph of Arimathea at Glastonbury* J. Clark 1955

Mac Cana, Proinsias. *Celtic Mythology* Hamlyn 1970

Mackenzie, Donald. A. *Ancient Man in Britain* 1912

Mackey, Albert. G. *Masonic Lexicon* Philadelphia 1869

Mc Naughton, Duncan. *A Scheme of Babylonian Chronology* Luzac 1930

Maspero, G. *The Dawn of Civilization* (On ancient Chaldea) S. P. C. K. 1894

Maunder, E. W. *The Astronomy of the Bible* The Epworth Press. London 1922

Meller, Walter, Clifford. *Old Times* T. Werner Laurie

Michell, John. *City of Revelation* Garnstone Press 1972

Michell, Roland. L. N. *Egyptian Calendar* Luzac 1900

Morgan, Owen. *The Light of Brittannia* Cardiff 1898

O'Brien, Henry. *The Round Towers of Ireland* London 1834

Ovenden, M. W. 'Origin of the Constellations' vol. 71.1960 - 61. No 3. *The Journal of the British Astronomical Association*

Owen, Robert. *Sanctorale Catholicum or Book of Saints* C. Kegan Paul. London 1880

Parsons, John Denham. *The Non-Christian Cross* Simpkin, Marshall, Hamilton, Kent & Co. London 1896

144

Pike, Albert. *Morals & Dogma* Charleston 1916

Powell, F. G. Montague. *Studies in the Lesser Mysteries* Theosophical Publishing House 1920

Pryce, John. *The Ancient British Church* Longmans Green. London 1878

Regardie, Israel. *The Golden Dawn* vol.3 The Aries Press. Chicago 1939

Rhys, John. 'Celtic Heathendom' Hibbert Lecture 1886

Robinson, J. Armitage. *Two Glastonbury Legends* Cambridge 1926

Rolleston, T. W. *Myths & Legends of the Celtic Race* Harrap

Sadler, Henry. *Masonic Facts & Fictions* Diprise & Bateman 1887

Schodde, G. H. *The Book of Enoch* trans. from Ethiopic. W. P. Draper. Andover. USA 1882

Seymour,W. W. *The Cross in Tradition & History of Art* Putnams 1898

Sharkey, John. *Celtic Mysteries* Thames & Hudson

Spence, Lewis. *Magic Arts in Celtic Britain* Rider

Spence, Lewis. *The Mysteries of Britain* Rider

Stukeley, W. *Abury* 1743

Squire, Charles. *Celtic Myth & Legend* Gresham Publishing

Toland, J. *History of the Druids* R. Huddleston. Montrose 1814

Vermaseren, M. J. *Mithras the Secret God* Chatto & Windus. London 1963

Vinycomb, John. *Fictitious & Symbolic Creatures in Art* Chapman Hall. London 1906

Voge, L. M. B. 'Heraldry' 2.vol 6. *The Comason*. 1914

Westcott, W. Wynn. *'Numbers' their Occult Power & Mystic Value* Theosophical Publishing Society. London 1890

Willetts, R. F. *Cretan Cults & Festivals* Routledge, Kegan, Paul. London 1962

Two local societies of interest:

Association Terre de Rhedae.
Le Reflet de la Fabuleuse Rhedae. (For English readers)
11190 Rennes le Château. Tel: 68.74.14.56.

Map of Our Valley →

Excerpts from I.G.N. Carte Topographique 2347 1:2500 East and West.
Rivers, Fountains, Sources, put in by hand.
Reproduced by permission of the National Geographic Institute of France.